Bible
Black Belts

Mark Burrows

Scripture quotations in this publication, unless otherwise indicated, are from the New Revised Standard
Version of the Bible, copyright 1989, Division of Christian Education of the National
Council of the Churches of Christ in the United States of America. Used by permission.
All rights reserved.

Scripture quotations noted CEB are taken from the Common English Bible. Copyright © 2011 by the
Common English Bible. All rights reserved. Used by permission.

Scripture quotations noted NIV are taken from the Holy Bible, NEW INTERNATIONAL
VERSION®. Copyright © 1973, 1978, 1984 by International Bible Society. All rights
reserved throughout the world. Used by permission of International Bible Society.

Scripture quotations noted KJV are taken from the King James or Authorized Version of the Bible.

Mark Burrows is a composer, a writer, and Director of Children's Ministries at First United Methodist Church, Fort
Worth, Texas, where he has served for fifteen years. Mark's published works include numerous best-sellers for several
publishers. For over six years, Mark wrote music and curriculum for *Children First, Wow Time!, PowerXpress!® Living God's
Word, Live B.I.G.®*, and *Exploring Faith®*. Part of his duties at First UMC include sharing the weekly Children's Message
and leading the monthly Children First service. He is also known to many little listeners as Mister Mark.
His three albums have won a total of nine awards.

ISBN: 978-1-4267-3092-4

PACP 00915504-01

Editor: Daphna Flegal
Production Editors: David Whitworth & Julie Glass
Designer: Gillian Housewright
Internal Photos: Mark Burrows

11 12 13 14 15 16 17 18 19 20—10 9 8 7 6 5 4 3 2 1

Printed in the U. S. A.

Contents

Tough Choices

So with all the inspired Scripture in the Bible, how does one choose the passages that make it into *Bible Black Belts* and those that don't? It's really, REALLY hard!

We started by asking dozens of parents, "What are some passages of Scripture that you like or have found particularly meaningful in your own life?" We asked several ministers and teachers the same question, as well as a follow-up, "What are some passages of Scripture that you feel every child should know?" We received a wide variety of offerings—well over one hundred different passages. And as you might imagine, some passages, such as the Twenty-third Psalm and John 3:16, were recommended by several people.

We noticed that many of the passages seemed to fit into certain categories. These categories helped us structure *Bible Black Belts,* so that at every belt level, the children would have an opportunity to learn a Scripture passage in each category.

Here are the categories we identified:

Words of Celebration — for moments of joy and wonder. We belong to an awesome God who is worthy of praise. "Make a joyful noise to the LORD, all the earth" (Psalm 100:1).

Words of Comfort — for moments of uncertainty, fear, even deep sadness. We belong to a caring God who loves us and is with us all the way. "Those who wait for the LORD shall renew their strength" (Isaiah 40:31).

Words of Inspiration — for times when we need to remember not only to reach up and reach in, but to reach out as well. We are wonderfully made, and with God's help, we can do great things. "You are the light of the world" (Matthew 5:14).

Words of Wisdom — for the specific times when we can benefit from a timeless life lesson. We belong to a gracious God. One of the best ways we can say thank you for all God gives us is to constantly strive to be our best selves. "To do righteousness and justice is more acceptable to the LORD than sacrifice" (Proverbs 21:3).

Words of Jesus — for all times. God gave us Jesus to teach us about the true nature of God's unending love. "Treat people in the same way that you want them to treat you" (Luke 6:31, CEB).

Aside from these categories, we also wanted the children to know some Bible basics, such as the books of the Old Testament in order, the books of the New Testament in order, and how to look up a Scripture. And we also felt the children should know some larger passages—the Ten Commandments and the parable of the Good Samaritan, for instance—without having to learn them word for word. Together, these Bible basics and larger passages were put into a category called "The Big Thing." There's one "Big Thing" for each belt level.

After structuring *Bible Black Belts* around these six categories, many wonderful, meaningful Scripture passages were left out (including some of my personal favorites). If your favorite Scripture was not included here in *Bible Black Belts,* not to worry. There's no reason why the children can't spend a new year earning their Second-Degree Bible Black Belt with all-new Scriptures!

Another difficult choice for us was which version/interpretation of Scripture to use. But the Bible's the Bible, right? Well . . .

In most cases we found that the New Revised Standard Version and the Common English Bible worked really well. And then there were passages, the Twenty-third Psalm and the Lord's Prayer in particular, where we simply couldn't resist the King James Version. We also found it interesting to see what an interpretation in more contemporary language—such as THE MESSAGE—looked and felt like.

Selecting the version of Scripture is a very personal matter. Please select the one you feel works best for your church setting and the children.

The Belts

One of the things the kids like the most about *Bible Black Belts* is, well, the belts. Depending on your budget, there are many options.

There are numerous martial arts supply companies that offer belts in a variety of colors and sizes. Many of these companies are online.

One relatively inexpensive option is to purchase fabric and make the belts yourself. I'm not exactly a sewing expert, but I was able to make a number of belts out of felt. Felt is durable and affordable, and one yard of felt (at 72 inches long) can easily make ten belts.

The belts can be hung on a rack in the dojo or stored in a large bin, or they may be taken home by the children between sessions.

At the beginning of the first session for a Belt Level, present the children with the belts they will be earning for that level, and collect the belts from the previous level. At the end of the entire *Bible Black Belts* program, you can have a special ceremony where all the children get to take their black belts home. Invite parents and other family members to the ceremony, and have the children demonstrate a few of their favorite Scripture activities. The children can keep the black belts while all the belts in the other colors are ready to be used the following year. That way you only have to replace the black belts.

This is different from martial arts, where a student wears the belt from the current level while working on the belt for the next level. For instance, a student would wear the brown belt while moving up to the black belt. However, this seemed confusing for the *Bible Black Belts* program.

Talk of "moving up" to the next belt level inevitably leads to some questions: What if a child doesn't have the verse memorized in time? Does that child still get to move up to the next belt level?

Those are excellent questions that we spent a lot of time grappling with. Here's what we decided to do.

We offer the Belt-Level activities for an entire month. At the beginning of the next month, every child gets to work on the next Belt Level.

We briefly considered the more hard-line approach of requiring a child to memorize all the Scriptures in a Belt Level before earning that belt. But then we considered some factors:

- A child misses a session due to illness or bad weather.

- A child misses a session because of an ill parent who can't drive the child to the church.

- A child's parents are no longer together and currently attend different churches. This child comes every other week.

- A child is a visitor and is already feeling like an outsider.

- The given activity for a Scripture doesn't gel with a child's optimal way of learning.

- A child has a learning difficulty which makes it challenging to memorize a passage of Scripture.

All of these factors, and many others, are very real possibilities. And none of them are the fault of the child. So at the beginning of the first session for a certain Belt Level, every child receives the belt for that level.

One option for recognizing those children who have dutifully memorized each passage could be to use colored stickers. For every passage memorized, place a sticker that corresponds to the color of the Belt Level on the inside cover of the child's Bible. That way the child has a visible record (that Mom and Dad can see) of his or her achievements, without having other children feel "left behind" by comparison.

The Belt Levels

A Belt Level is a group of Scriptures or Bible skills the children must learn in order to attain the colored belt for that level. There are nine belt levels in all: white, yellow, orange, green, blue, purple, red, brown, and black. The children begin the first month wearing the white belts.

Each Belt Level contains six different passages of Scripture or Bible skills. That doesn't necessarily mean that a child must learn all six passages in order to earn that belt. If you can only squeeze fifteen minutes of *Bible Black Belts* into each week, perhaps the children will find it challenging enough to learn "The Big Thing," plus one or two other passages of Scripture. That's just fine. The "Bible Black Belts Police" aren't going to come out to your church and shut down your dojo. Do what works best for your setting and keeps the kids excited about exploring Scripture.

The Living-Word Dojo

Where Scripture Comes to Life

Dojo is a Japanese word meaning "place of the way." While it is most often associated with martial arts training, it can apply to other places where formal training occurs.

Here is a basic checklist for setting up a Living-Word Dojo in your church.

- Look for a room with as much open space as possible.

- Keep a few chairs in the room which can be set aside until needed.

- Have several Bibles on hand.

- Put up a rack for holding the current set of belts.

- Have a large bin for storing the belts not in use.

- Keep a few wooden writing boards (not for breaking) which can be easily stored away.

- Make a sign with the words to Psalm 119:105: "Your word is a lamp to my feet and a light to my path" (see page 109). This can be put above the main entrance.

- Stock a supply bin with the following: masking tape, crayons, markers (for older children), pencils, scissors, index cards, card stock, adhesive putty, yarn, a paper punch, two beanbags, a ball, balloons.

- Keep a CD player or MP3 player on hand.

If you choose, you can provide carpet squares or rattan mats for the children to sit on. Anything else you want to do to give it more of a "dojo vibe" is totally up to you.

Almost all of this can be easily packed up and stowed away if the dojo is set up in a room that is used for other purposes throughout the week.

Bible Black Belts

Solid content. Fun, engaging activities. It's quite the balancing act. Lean too far to one side and we hear, "Our children need more Bible! They know how to make an origami dove, but they don't know the Twenty-third Psalm." Go too far the other way and we get, "My kids just aren't having fun. They have to sit still in desks all week."

Both sides make really good points. I've seen (and taught) plenty of lessons that were fun and action-packed, but the supposed scriptural theme couldn't be found. And I've seen plenty of lessons that were full of Bible content—historical information, translations of the original Hebrew, and so on—but were drier than toast!

When I first started developing *Bible Black Belts,* it wasn't simply as a "fresh new take" on Bible curriculum. It was developed as what I saw to be truly needed:

- For parents who want their children to have a foundation in Bible basics.

- For parents who want their children dragging them to church, not the other way around.

- For teachers who are looking for a program that offers a healthy balance of fun and content.

- For children who are made to "sit still and be quiet" way too much of their lives.

- For my own church's desperate need for a program that not only teaches children The Story, but teaches them that they are part of The Story.

I'm no expert in martial arts (or anything else, really) but I can certainly appreciate the outstanding model they provide for connecting physical, mental, and emotional development into one. And let's face it—kids think it's way cool!

Reflect, Connect, Respect

We want our children to do more than memorize. We want them to internalize. For too many kids, the Bible is just about "a bunch of things that happened way back when to bearded guys in robes."

One of the most important things we can do to counteract this is give our children the time and space to reflect on the passages of Scripture they're learning.

Each category section in *Bible Black Belts* is accompanied by **For Reflection**—a question or idea that relates directly to the theme of the Scripture.

- After completing an activity, invite the children to sit with you on the floor in a circle.

- Take in a few deep, cleansing breaths.

- Read the For Reflection question/idea.

- Have the children sit quietly for a minute and reflect. **Reflect**

- Then have the children divide into pairs and share their reflections (as much as they are comfortable) with their partners. **Connect**

- As the children connect with one another, encourage attentive listening. Also, we want to make sure the children know they are in the "judgment-free zone." This isn't the time for disagreements about interpretation of a passage of Scripture. It's a time for listening and understanding. **Respect**

Make sure you allow plenty of time for this. It would be easy to spend all the time in a session on the activities and run out of time for this "extra." But **Reflect, Connect, Respect** is very important. While activities may give the children ways to remember the Scripture, **Reflect, Connect, Respect** may well give them the reasons for learning the Scripture.

The Activities

While there are many games in *Bible Black Belts,* not every activity is a game. Some of the activities are contemplative in nature. Some are very physical. Some are even humorous. Each activity was designed or selected to connect with a particular Bible skill or Scripture passage. In this way the activity does more than simply make Scripture learning more fun. It actually serves as a memory aide. For instance, the accompanying activity for a passage on unending love may be an Infinity Walk.

And no two Scriptures utilize the same activity, in an effort, once again, to make each activity more directly helpful in the memorization of a particular passage of Scripture.

You may want to look at *Words of Comfort* from the Black Belt Level (page 103) as you begin the program. This activity is a simple, and valuable, activity that you can use throughout the year. *Bible Black Belts* is highly active. From time to time, you may find that the room is perhaps a bit too active (or loud). Teach the children this simple call and response using Psalm 46:10 to help get their attention and bring stillness to the room.

The Possibilities

Bible Black Belts was originally designed to be a series of one-hour sessions for use in Sunday school over the course of nine months. But there are many other possibilities as well. Below are a few session options with approximate timings of the activities.

Option 1—60-Minute Session

5 minutes	1. Children enter, put on their belts, and find a place to sit on the floor.
1 minute	2. Recite the *Bible Black Belts Pledge*.
5 minutes	3. Review an activity and Scripture from a previous session. This needs to be a simple, no-setup-required activity, based on a short passage of Scripture. The idea is to get the kids feeling confident and successful right from the start, while making sure that a Scripture memorized in an earlier session is still memorized.
10 minutes	4. An activity for one of the shorter Scripture passages for that belt level.
13-16 minutes	5. An activity for "The Big Thing" for that belt level.
8 minutes	6. An activity for one of the shorter Scripture passages for that belt level.
5 minutes	7. Reflect-Connect-Respect. It is important to do this here so the children can more easily reflect on the Scriptures for that particular belt level. Also, it gives you the flexibility to allow the children to take more time with this if you feel there is some truly meaningful reflection and connection going on.
7-10 minutes	8. Review an activity and Scripture from a previous session. This needs to be different from the first review (#3). If there is time, review more than one Scripture and activity. At this point in the session, things need to move a little quicker, with less time spent on each activity.
1 minute	9. Closing prayer.
2 minutes	10. Children put away their belts, straighten up the dojo, and leave.

The 60-minute session is an ideal option for the Sunday school hour. You can start with the White Belt Level in September and move to a new belt level each month, concluding with the Black Belt Level in May. This is how *Bible Black Belts* was originally designed, and it takes in to account special times of year. The Green Belt Level, which would occur in December, contains Scriptures specific to Advent and Christmas. Both the Purple Belt Level (February) and Red Belt Level (March) contain Scriptures appropriate for Lent. And the months with relatively less to memorize are December and May, when other activities, both at church and at school, tend to increase.

Option 2—45-Minute Session

3 minutes	1.	Children enter, put on their belts, and sit on the floor.
1 minute	2.	Recite the *Bible Black Belts Pledge*.
4 minutes	3.	Review an activity and Scripture from a previous session.
10 minutes	4.	An activity for one of the shorter Scripture passages for that belt level.
15 minutes	5.	An activity for "The Big Thing" for that belt level.
6 minutes	6.	An activity for one of the shorter Scripture passages for that belt level.
3 minutes	7.	Reflect-Connect-Respect. It is important to do this here so that the children can more easily reflect on the Scriptures for that particular belt level. Also, it gives you the flexibility to allow the children to take more time with this if there is some truly meaningful reflection and connection going on.
1 minute	8	Closing prayer.
2 minutes	9.	Children put away their belts, straighten up the dojo, and leave.

The 45-minute session works great as a Wednesday or Sunday evening option that can serve as a great companion piece to other children's programming such as choir rehearsal. Notice that for many of the activities, less time has been allotted. And the second review session has been left out entirely. But there is still plenty of time for the children to experience many activities and Scriptures. And 45 minutes is a good fit for younger elementary.

Option 3—15-Minute Session

1 minute	1. Recite the *Bible Black Belts Pledge*.
3-4 minutes	2. Review an activity and Scripture from a previous session.
6-7 minutes	3. An activity for "The Big Thing" for that belt level.
2-3 minutes	4. Reflect-Connect-Respect.
1 minute	5. Closing prayer.

If you would like to initiate a *Bible Black Belts* program, but do not want to use it as the sole curriculum for Sunday school, consider this option. *Bible Black Belts* can occur the last fifteen minutes of each Sunday school hour.

Many churches hold two or more worship services, with 15 to 30 minutes between services. The 15-minute session is a great option for keeping children engaged during that tricky in-between time.

Note: Aside from regular weekly sessions, you could make *Bible Black Belts* the focus of a weeklong church camp during the summer or spring break.

Bible Black Belts Pledge

This is the Bible—the book of God's love.

It is full of amazing stories of faith,
amazing people of faith,
and amazing deeds of faith.

The Bible may have been written long ago,
but it has great meaning in my life today!

Its words can inspire me,
comfort me,
teach me,
and challenge me to be my best self—
a true servant of God.

The Bible is not a weapon.
I will not throw it at anyone.
I will not use its words to hurt others
just so I can feel better about myself.

This is the Bible—the book of God's love.

White Belt Level

The Big Thing: Bible Black Belts Pledge; Bible skills—finding book, chapter, and verse in the Old Testament books Genesis–Deuteronomy

Words of Celebration: Genesis 1:31

Words of Comfort: Romans 8:38-39

Words of Inspiration: Psalm 119:105

Words of Wisdom: Ecclesiastes 3:1

Words of Jesus: Luke 6:41, CEB

The Big Thing

Bible Black Belts Pledge

Say the **Bible Black Belts Pledge** (page 15).

• Activity—Words in Motion

Divide the children into five groups.

Invite each group to create actions to use when reciting each of the sections of the Bible Black Belts Pledge. (The first and last sections of the pledge are the same, so one group will be responsible for both of those sections.) For example, Group 2 could incorporate the following actions:

It is full of amazing stories of faith, — *Pantomime reading a book.*
Amazing people of faith, — *Bring your thumbs toward your chest to indicate self.*
And amazing deeds of faith. — *Flex your muscles.*

Once each group has created actions, bring all the children together. Have each group teach their motions to the others as they recite their part of the pledge.

Then invite the children to perform all the actions in sequence as they recite the entire *Bible Black Belts Pledge* (page 15) together.

The children may perform these actions each week as they say their *Bible Black Belts Pledge*. You may also choose to have them create new actions halfway through the year or whenever you feel things need to be "freshened up" a bit.

This activity incorporates many memorization techniques, including repetition, peer mentoring, imagination, vivid imagery, and (depending on the children in the room) humor.

Bible Skills

Look up passages of Scripture by book, chapter, and verse.

• Activity—Look It Up

Supplies: Bibles, large sheet of paper or markerboard, markers

This is not one of the most physical activities. But it helps foster the important skill of being able to find a passage of Scripture.

Make sure each child in the room has access to a Bible. It is a good idea to keep plenty of Bibles on hand.

One of the first things most of us learn about the Bible is that it is more than one book. It is a collection of many books—almost like a library.

Have the children locate the table of contents in their Bibles. Most Bibles should have a table of contents that lists the books of the Old Testament and New Testament.

Ask: How many books are in the Old Testament?

Say: When you think you know, tap your nose.

When most, if not all, of the children are tapping their noses, invite one of the children to offer the answer. *(39)* It is important to keep an eye out for those who may need help.

Ask: How many books are in the New Testament?

Have the children follow the same procedure. *(27)*

Ask: So how many books are there in the Bible altogether? *(66)*

The children will need to become comfortable with their Bibles. They will be looking up multiple Scripture passages in each session.

Say: When looking up a passage of Scripture, we need to know three things—the particular book of the Bible, the chapter, and the verse. This is like the "address" where each Scripture "lives."

The name of the book of the Bible comes first.

Each book is divided into chapters. The number of the chapter comes right after the name of the book.

Each chapter is divided into verses. This number comes after the chapter number. In most Bibles, the chapter numbers are printed larger than the verse numbers.

Write an example where all the children can see it. Example: Genesis 1:31.

Ask: What is the book where this Scripture can be found? *(Genesis)*
What is the chapter? *(1)* What is the verse? *(31)*

Invite the children to find this Scripture passage in their Bibles. Some children will find it very quickly. Others will need more time. Allow all the children to find the Scripture.

Have one child read the passage. Then have all the children read the passage together.

Repeat this activity numerous times with different verses. Don't be in too big a hurry. This is a foundation skill that the children will need throughout. A few extra minutes spent up front could save you hours later on.

If, however, it becomes apparent that all but one or two children are able to find Scripture passages quickly, consider sitting next to that child. When it is time to look up a passage of Scripture, hold your Bible where the child can easily see it. Go slowly and deliberately through the steps of locating the Scripture. There's no need to say anything aloud unless the child specifically asks you. Simply model the steps.

For the first session, stick with passages in the first five books of the Bible (the Torah). Later, work up to all the books of the Old Testament, then the entire Bible.

Rather than just have the children look up random passages of Scripture, have them find passages that they will learn throughout the course of *Bible Black Belts*.

As a follow-up activity, you can ask questions that require the children to use their Bible skills in order to answer.

Some examples:

> **Ask:** How many chapters are there in Genesis? *(50)*
> How many verses are there in Exodus, chapter 4? *(31)*
> Does Numbers have an even or odd number of chapters? *(even)*
> Which book comes after Exodus? *(Leviticus)*
> What is the fifth book of the Old Testament? *(Deuteronomy)*

• For Reflection
> **Ask:** When was the last time you read something from the Bible?
> Not including the Bible, what is your favorite book?

Words of Celebration

God saw everything that he had made, and indeed, it was very good.

Genesis 1:31

• Activity—Living Creation Sculptures

Supplies: Bibles, index cards, marker

Prepare six index cards, each with one of the days of Creation on it, and a brief description of what was created.

Day 1 — *day and night*
Day 2 — *the sky (often called the firmament, the dome that separates the waters above from the waters below)*
Day 3 — *the land, the seas, and the plants*
Day 4 — *the sun and moon*
Day 5 — *the creatures of the sea and the birds of the air*
Day 6 — *all the creatures on land, including man and woman*

Divide the children into groups of three, and give each group an index card. Instruct the children to not share the contents of their cards with anyone outside their groups.

Have groups each find an open space in which to work. One child in each group will be the sculptor. The other two will follow the sculptor's instructions and allow themselves to be sculpted—not turned into pretzels, just part of a living sculpture. The goal of the sculptor is to pose the other two children in such a way that they represent the day of creation indicated on that group's card. For example, if the group has the card for Day 5, the sculptor might have one child spread her arms out like wings and have the other child use his hands to make a tail fin and a dorsal fin.

Once all the groups have had a chance to practice forming the living-creation sculptures, invite them all to sit down in a row or two on the floor.

Then call up one of the groups, and have the sculptor form the other two children into the living-creation sculpture. The others must guess which day of Creation is being represented by the sculpture. Allow all the groups a chance to show their sculptures to the others.

Every time the children guess the day of Creation represented by the sculpture, all the children should say the Genesis 1:31 passage aloud in unison.

Once all the groups have had a chance, collect the cards, shuffle them, and hand them back out to the groups. Each group must have a different child of the three be the sculptor.

Repeat this again so that all three children in each group get to be the sculptor. If a group gets the same card twice, encourage the new sculptor to think how he or she could still make the sculpture look different.

You can even have the children try a couple of variations on the activity. One variation—the children being sculpted must be perfectly still when in their places. Another variation—allow the sculptures to move and make sounds.

• For Reflection
Ask: What do you think is the most amazing thing God created?
God saw that all of it was good. Is there any plant or animal that you have a hard time seeing as good?

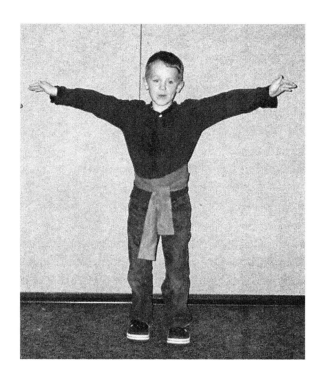

Words of Comfort

For I am convinced that neither death, nor life, nor angels, nor rulers, nor things present, nor things to come, nor powers, nor height, nor depth, nor anything else in all creation, will be able to separate us from the love of God in Christ Jesus our Lord.

Romans 8:38-39

• Activity—Scripture Pass

Supplies: Bibles, index cards, pencils, beanbag or cushioned ball

Provide the children with ten index cards and pencils to write the following phrases from the Scripture, one phrase per card. It is a good idea to also number the cards on the back, 1-10.

Card 1 — *neither death*
Card 2 — *nor life*
Card 3 — *nor angels*
Card 4 — *nor rulers*
Card 5 — *nor things present*
Card 6 — *nor things to come*
Card 7 — *nor powers*
Card 8 — *nor height*
Card 9 — *nor depth*
Card 10 — *nor anything else in all creation*

Have the children stand in a circle. Take up the cards.

Talk through the Scripture a couple of times.

Shuffle the cards and distribute them to the children in the circle. If you have fewer than ten children, consider doubling up some of the parts of Scripture onto fewer cards. If you have more than ten children, they can take turns. If you have a lot more than ten, make two circles. Have the children hold the cards with the numbers facing out toward the others.

Hand a beanbag or cushioned ball to the child holding Card 1—"neither death." As you do this, say, "For I am convinced that . . ." When the child holding Card 1 receives the beanbag, he or she says what is on the card, "neither death."

Now here's the trick: this child must now pass the ball to the child with the card that says "nor life." That child could be right next to the first child or that child could be on the other side of the circle. When the second child catches the beanbag, he or she says the phrase on the card. And so on. Once the beanbag has made its complete circuit, ending with the child holding Card 10, all the children continue reciting the Scripture, ". . . will be able to separate us from the love of God in Christ Jesus our Lord."

The first time through the game, it may be necessary to rely on the numbers on each card to keep things in order. But as you continue to play, after several times try to move away from the numbers so that the children are only using each other and the Scripture itself to pass the ball in the right order.

This is a very useful game for many different Scriptures. It works especially well for this one because there is a long list of similar things, and this game helps with the sequence.

After several rounds, take up the cards, shuffle them, redistribute, and play again.

• For Reflection
Ask: Have you ever been far away from loved ones? *(For example: Do you have grandparents who live far away? Have you ever spent several days away from your parents at camp?)*
Did you feel that they still loved you?

Words of Inspiration

Your word is a lamp to my feet and a light to my path.
Psalm 119:105

• Activity—Making a Scripture Path

Supplies: Bibles, colored card stock or construction paper, black markers or crayons, pencils, safety scissors

Divide the children into pairs. Give each pair six sheets of colored card stock or construction paper, two black markers or crayons, and two pairs of (reasonably safe) scissors. Make sure that the six pieces of card stock the pair receives are a single color, but that each pair has a different color than the other pairs have. (If need be, you can modify this by handing out white card stock to all, but a different color of marker or crayon to each pair.)

Instruct the pairs to use the card stock to make six large footprints. They may trace their own shoes onto the card stock, in which case you will need to supply pencils as well. You don't want to have to face the parent whose child just got black marker all over their brand-new Sunday shoes.

Make sure each pair makes three right footprints and three left footprints. Inside each footprint, they must write a different portion of the Scripture.

> **Footprint 1:** *Your word*
> **Footprint 2:** *is a lamp*
> **Footprint 3:** *to my feet*
> **Footprint 4:** *and a light*
> **Footprint 5:** *to my path.*
> **Footprint 6:** *Psalm 119:105*

Once the children have done this, they may carefully cut out the footprints and then return scissors, markers, and pencils to you. Each pair should now have six footprints in their own distinct color.

That's the prep work; now it's time for the game.

Have one child in each pair close her or his eyes.

The other child must take the footprints and place them around the room so that they make a path. The path can be straight, crooked, simple, crazy, however they want to make it. Just please, no footprints on top of furniture or humans. Once that is done, the floor should have many colored paths, one for each pair.

At your signal, the children with their eyes closed may open them and locate the first footprint in the Scripture path. They must pick up that footprint and say the portion of Scripture written on it.

Then they must find the next footprint in their Scripture path. They must go in Scripture order. It isn't enough to gather, say, all the red footprints. The first player to complete the Scripture path wins for that team. Once all the children have completed their Scripture paths, have the partners switch roles and play again.

It will only take a couple of times before the children catch on that the closer they put their footprints together, the more likely they will win. So after a couple of rounds, have the children go through the motions of one partner closing her or his eyes while the other places the footprints around the room. But this time, have the children with their eyes closed keep their eyes closed for a few more seconds. Then you reassign the paths. Tap one of the children whose eyes are closed and say, "This time, you won't follow the blue path, but the red one." Do this for all the other children whose eyes are closed. You only have to do this a couple of times to keep the kids on their toes.

By the way, I could have made the footprints before the children arrived. But writing something down is a big memorization tool. When I hand the children something pre-made rather than having them make it themselves, I deprive them of a golden memorization opportunity.

• For Reflection

Ask: Have you ever had to make a tough choice between something you wanted to do and something you felt was right to do?

How could studying the Bible and learning about God's teachings help you make the tough choices?

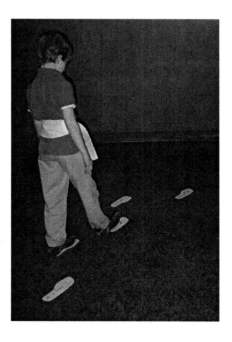

Words of Wisdom

For everything there is a season,
and a time for every matter under heaven.

Ecclesiastes 3:1

• Activity—Human Clock Game

Supplies: Bibles, card stock, markers, posterboard or large sheet of paper

Prepare twelve pieces of card stock with the numbers 1-12.

Have the children think of some common activities and the times they happen. Write these down on posterboard or a large sheet of paper so that all the children can see. It isn't necessary to put A.M. or P.M.

Some examples:
Lunch — 12:00
Dance Practice — 5:30
Children's Chapel — 9:45
Bedtime — 8:30
My Favorite Show — 4:00

And so on. Make sure that each activity has its own distinct time.

Next, have twelve children sit in a very wide circle on the floor. Hand one of the numbered cards to each child so that the numbers appear as they do on a clock (you know, before digital clocks).

Choose two more children to be the "minute hand" and the "hour hand." The child representing the minute hand can hold her or his arms straight overhead to look longer than the hour hand.

Have the two clock hands stand in the center of the circle.

Call out an activity from the posted list.

The minute hand and hour hand must arrange themselves on the giant human clock to show the time that particular activity takes place. They can lie on the floor with their feet touching the center and their heads toward the numbers. (You may want to mark the center of the clock with a piece of tape on the floor.)

Once they have shown the correct time, have them switch places with two children in the circle. Allow each child a chance to be a minute hand or hour hand.

Here's a wrinkle you can add that will make the game more challenging while helping with memorization. As soon as an activity has been called out, the children in the circle start chanting the Ecclesiastes 3:1 passage at a moderate tempo. The minute hand and hour hand must get in the correct positions before the children in the circle finish reciting the Scripture.

If you don't have twelve children in the room, simply place the numbered cards on the floor to look like a giant clock. If you have more than twelve, the children can take turns. If you have a lot more than twelve, consider assembling another clock.

• For Reflection

Ask: How much time each day do you spend doing school work?
How much time each day do you spend playing? eating? sleeping? visiting with friends and family? praying? helping others?

Words of Jesus

*Why do you see the splinter in your brother's or sister's eye
but don't notice the log in your own eye?*

Luke 6:41, CEB

• Activity—Who Am I?
Supplies: Bibles, self-adhesive nametags or self-adhesive notes, markers

Prepare several self-adhesive nametags (Post-it® notes will work fine) with the names of several well-known Bible figures—people and even animals. Limit the number of choices for younger children.

Here is a sample list:

Noah	Moses
Mary	Zacchaeus
David	Goliath
Jonah	Samson
Pharaoh	Adam
Eve	Daniel
Queen Esther	Angel
Shepherd	Carpenter
Fisherman	Donkey
Camel	Sheep

Have the children sit in a circle. Place a nametag on each child's back, between the shoulders. This way, they won't be able to see their own nametags. (By the way, cover any mirrors that might be in the room. Kids are pretty resourceful.)

Invite the children to stand and wander about the room. They can strike up a conversation with whomever they like, preferably with many people over the course of several minutes. Every child must talk to the other children as if these others are who their nametags identify them to be, but must not ever mention the actual names on the nametags.

Example 1: Child A can say to Child B, "You look nice and strong. I wonder if you could help me open this jar. By the way, I notice you haven't had a haircut in quite some time. I have a barber I could recommend." Who is Child B? (*Samson*)

Example 2: Child C says to Child D, "You sure are a wee little man. Was that you I saw up in a sycamore tree the other day?" Who is Child D? (*Zacchaeus*)

The goal is for each child to guess the name on her/his own nametag in as short a time as possible.

Once everyone has guessed the names on their own nametags, have all the children recite the Luke 6:41 Scripture. If time allows, let the children play another round or two. At the conclusion of each round, always have the children recite the Scripture.

Isn't it interesting how we can often see more in others than we do in ourselves?

• For Reflection

Ask: Have you ever been irritated by something someone did or said, only to realize later that you have done or said the same thing?

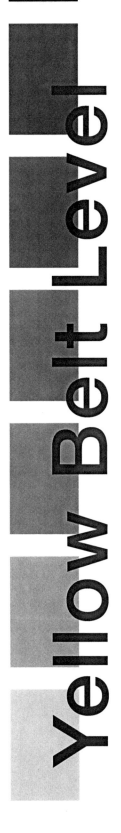

Yellow Belt Level

The Big Thing: Bible Black Belts Pledge, names of Old Testament books

Words of Celebration: Psalm 100:1-2

Words of Comfort: Jeremiah 29:11

Words of Inspiration: Ruth 1:16

Words of Wisdom: Proverbs 17:17

Words of Jesus: The Golden Rule—Luke 6:31, CEB

The Books of the Old Testament

Law

Genesis
Exodus
Leviticus
Numbers
Deuteronomy

History

Joshua
Judges
Ruth
1 Samuel
2 Samuel
1 Kings
2 Kings
1 Chronicles
2 Chronicles
Ezra
Nehemiah
Esther

Poetry

Job
Psalms
Proverbs
Ecclesiastes
Song of Solomon

Major Prophets

Isaiah
Jeremiah
Lamentations
Ezekiel
Daniel

Minor Prophets

Hosea
Joel
Amos
Obadiah
Jonah
Micah
Nahum
Habakkuk
Zephaniah
Haggai
Zechariah
Malachi

Fast Facts

- There are 39 books in the Old Testament.
- In the Jewish faith, the first five books are known as the Torah, which means "teaching."
- The Old Testament can be divided into five parts: Law, History, Poetry, Major Prophets, and Minor Prophets.
- The Major Prophets are so called because they wrote more than the others.
- While called "Law," the first five books of the Old Testament also contain a great deal of the history of God's people.
- The books of Poetry are also referred to as books of Wisdom because many of these passages of Scripture are filled with wise sayings and teachings.

By the way, keep in mind that these fast facts should be just that—fast. Many well-meaning Christian educators have spent so much time explaining the fascinating details of Bible background that they found themselves short on time for the actual Bible. If some of these facts can help the children keep all 39 books of the Old Testament straight, great. Otherwise, don't bog.

The Big Thing

Bible Black Belts Pledge
Say the **Bible Black Belts Pledge** (page 15).

• Activity—Genesis to Jumping Jacks
Supplies: Bibles

This game is a pentathlon . . . of sorts. As I was going through the books of the Old Testament, I was struck by how often the number five came up—five sections to the Old Testament, five books of Poetry, five books of the Major Prophets, even the first five books being known as the Pentateuch.

Have the children stand with you in the room. Make sure there is plenty of open space. Assign a different physical exercise to each of the five sections of the Old Testament. Here is a sample.

> **The five books of Law** — *Do five pushups.*
> **The twelve books of History** — *Hop in place twelve times.*
> **The five books of Poetry** — *Swim in place for five strokes.*
> **The five books of the Major Prophets** — *Dribble a pretend ball in place five times, switching hands for each dribble.*
> **The twelve books of the Minor Prophets** — *Do twelve jumping jacks.*

You could also ask the children to suggest exercises, such as jumping on one foot, knee bends, or jogging in place.

Once you have assigned an exercise for each of the five main sections, have the children recite the books out loud in sync with the exercises.

It is a good idea to take this one section at a time. Get all five books of Law and their corresponding exercise firmly internalized before moving on to the twelve books of History.

Once the children have learned each section, try putting all five sections together into an Old Testament pentathlon. And keep the exercise for each section consistent. This will help with memorization.

If you find that the kiddos are really solid on the order of the books, challenge them to perform the entire pentathlon . . . backwards! We want our children to be able to find the Book of Obadiah without mentally having to start at Genesis and go through all thirty books before getting there.

Here's an extension activity that also works as a quiz. Call out a book of the Old Testament. The children must indicate which of the five main sections contains that particular book by performing the corresponding exercise for that section. You can have the children do this one at a time for a more competitive version of the activity, or as a group for a cooperative version.

Be open to modifying some of the physical exercises for children who may not be able to do some of the ones listed. Perhaps try a pentathlon where each "exercise" must be performed while seated in a chair.

• For Reflection
Ask: When you go to the library, do you have a favorite section or do you like to explore many different sections? The next time you're in a library, see how long it takes you to find your favorite book.

Words of Celebration

Make a joyful noise to the LORD, all the earth.
Worship the LORD with gladness; come into his presence with singing.

Psalm 100:1-2

• Activity—Air Guitar

Supplies: Bibles

Have the children stand with you in a circle. Speak the Scripture together several times.

Next, choose one child to speak the first verse of the Scripture while playing an "air instrument" of her or his choice, such as air guitar, air drums, air sax, air accordion, and so on. The other children must respond by speaking the second verse of the Scripture while playing the same air instrument demonstrated by the first child. Allow each child the chance to lead in this activity.

After all the children have had a chance to lead, hold one monster "air-jam session." Invite the children to choose whichever air instrument they like. They are then to play their chosen instruments while speaking both verses of the Scripture in unison. Do this three times, getting louder each time. (No stage-diving, please.)

• For Reflection

Ask: Have you ever been so happy about something that you couldn't express it in words? How did you express your happiness?

Words of Comfort

For surely I know the plans I have for you, says the LORD,
plans for your welfare and not for harm,
to give you a future with hope.

Jeremiah 29:11

• Activity—A Path of Hope

Supplies: Bibles; paper punch; several 12-foot lengths of yarn, each one a different color;
index cards, eight cards for each length of yarn; several pencils

Use a paper punch to make a hole in each index card.

Divide the children into pairs. Give each pair a length of yarn, and each child four index cards and a pencil.

Have the children write a different word of comfort, affirmation, or inspiration on each card. Here are a few choices:

Hope	Love	Joy
Patience	Peace	Compassion
Comfort	Laughter	Dreams
Music	Friends	Yes
Togetherness		

Once all the cards have been made, have one child in each pair close her or his eyes. The other person must make a path using the length of yarn. The path can be straight, winding, a spiral, several right angles, however the child wants to make it. Along the way, about every three feet, the child should thread one of the cards on the yarn. Do not tie these onto the yarn. They will stay in place just fine.

Then have the children whose eyes are closed open their eyes and walk along their Path of Hope. As they walk along and see a card on the path, they should stop, read the card, think about that word for a few seconds, then move on, leaving the card where it is.

When a child has finished walking the path, have her or him wait silently until all have completed their Path of Hope. Then invite everyone to join in reciting Jeremiah 29:11 together.

Next, have the partners switch roles. The new path-makers can create completely different paths using the four cards that they made.

At the end of this session, each child gives the cards he or she made to the partner to take home.

This activity can be modified in any number of ways. The lengths of yarn can be much longer, and even more cards can be used.

Some children may do better with pictures. There is no reason the children can't draw pictures to express comforting, affirming, inspiring ideas, if words do not come easily.

Also, don't feel the need for each path to be tidily self-contained. Very often in life, our Path of Hope crosses the paths of others.

• For Reflection

Ask: Do you think God plans every step of your life? Do you think God wants the best for you and gives you the freedom to make your own decisions? How do you think God works in your life?

Words of Inspiration

Where you go, I will go; where you lodge, I will lodge;
your people shall be my people, and your God my God.

Ruth 1:16

• Activity—Find the Leader

Supplies: Bibles

This is a simple and fun game to play. Choose one child to leave the room for just a few seconds. This child is "IT."

While that child is out, select another child to be the leader. That child must perform a repetitive activity, such as jogging in place, doing jumping jacks, hopping on one foot, stretching, playing air guitar, and so on. All the other children must do exactly what the leader is doing. Encourage the leader to switch activities often. Every time the leader switches, the other children must switch too.

Now here's the catch: you are going to bring the other child back in from outside. This child will get to watch the children carefully and try to guess which one is the leader. So naturally, there is some strategy involved. The child who is the leader doesn't want to switch activities when IT is looking right at her or him. And the other children don't want to look right at the leader. Otherwise, it won't take IT long to figure out who the leader is. And the main thing is for the children to stay together and in sync as much as possible.

Once the child who is IT has had up to three guesses, switch to a new leader and a new IT. Every time you switch children, have the entire group recite the Scripture.

For an added challenge, consider having the children recite the Scripture over and over while they perform the actions.

Allow each child a chance to be the leader and IT.

• For Reflection

Ask: Can you think of someone who is not a relative, but who you think of as family? What makes that person feel like a family member to you?

Words of Wisdom

A friend loves at all times, and kinsfolk are born to share adversity.

Proverbs 17:17

• Activity—Balloon Relay

Supplies: Bibles, balloons (two per child), masking tape

Blow up several balloons before the children arrive, two per child. If any children have latex allergies, provide a substitute, such as beach balls.

Clear the floor of any obstructions.

Place a long line of tape along the floor on one side of the room (the start line) and another line of tape on the opposite end (the finish line).

Divide the children into pairs. Have the pairs all go together to the start line.

Give each pair four balloons. The pairs must work as a team to carry each balloon one at a time from the start line to the finish line. Here's the catch: each child may only use one fingertip to touch the balloon. In other words, it's going to take both children working together to transport each of the balloons across the finish line. (The best way is for each child to touch the balloon from opposite sides and press in slightly. This will allow them to grip the balloon and pick it up. Then they must walk together to the finish line.)

And here's the other wrinkle: before the children can take each balloon, they must recite the Scripture in call-and-response.

> **Child 1:** A friend loves at all times,
> **Child 2:** and kinsfolk are born to share adversity.

Practice the Scripture with all the children together before playing the game. On your signal, the children may begin. The first team to get all four balloons across the finish line wins.

• For Reflection

Ask: Have you ever had to do work so difficult that it made you feel discouraged? How would you feel if, all of a sudden, a family member or friend offered to help you?

Words of Jesus

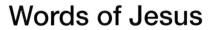

Treat people in the same way that you want them to treat you.
The Golden Rule—Luke 6:31, CEB

• Activity—Feel the Beat
Supplies: Bibles

Have the children sit with you on the floor in a circle. After reading Luke 6:31 aloud, have the children repeat it a few times. This is a short passage, and can be memorized quickly.

Divide the children into pairs. Have the partners sit facing one another. One child must hold out her or his hands with the palms facing up and close her or his eyes. The other child must lightly tap a simple rhythm into the palms of the other child's hands.

The rhythm could consist of:
    1 beat in the left hand and two beats in the right hand.
    4 beats in the left hand and 4 beats in the right hand.
    3 beats in both hands simultaneously.
    Any other combination.

It does not have to be a steady rhythm. It just needs to be simple and somewhat short. No twelve-beat rhythms, please.

Once the rhythm has been tapped into the palms (Treat people in the same way), that child may open her or his eyes. This child then tries to tap the exact same rhythm into her or his partner's palms (that you want them to treat you).

If the correct rhythm is repeated, then the partners switch roles. If the rhythm is off slightly, then the partner doing the tapping can give the other child one more try. Challenge the children to play this game as quietly as possible. And make sure the children are not slapping their partner's hands.

Play a few rounds and then have the children change partners. As they change, have the children speak the Scripture in unison.

• For Reflection
Ask: When was a time you did something really nice for someone, but that person didn't return the favor? If you could go back, would you still have done something nice for that person?

Treat people in the same way that you want them to treat you.

The Golden Rule—Luke 6:31, CEB

Orange Belt Level

The Big Thing: Bible Black Belts Pledge, names of New Testament books

Words of Celebration: Philippians 4:4

Words of Comfort: Revelation 21:4

Words of Inspiration: Matthew 5:14-16, CEB

Words of Wisdom: Galatians 5:22-23, CEB

Words of Jesus: John 15:12

The Books of the New Testament

Gospels	History	Letters (Epistles)	Prophecy
Matthew	Acts of the Apostles	Romans	Revelation
Mark		1 Corinthians	
Luke		2 Corinthians	
John		Galatians	
		Ephesians	
		Philippians	
		Colossians	
		1 Thessalonians	
		2 Thessalonians	
		1 Timothy	
		2 Timothy	
		Titus	
		Philemon	
		Hebrews	
		James	
		1 Peter	
		2 Peter	
		1 John	
		2 John	
		3 John	
		Jude	

Fast Facts

- There are 27 books in the New Testament.
- The first four books of the New Testament are known as the Gospels, meaning "good news." They tell of the life, ministry, death, and resurrection of Jesus.
- The first three Gospels are called the Synoptic Gospels because they share many of the same stories (syn = together; optic = view).
- There are 21 Epistles, or Letters.
- While many of these letters were written by the apostle Paul, the number is less than people once believed.
- To this day, scholars still don't agree on who wrote which letters.

As with the fast facts that accompany the books of the Old Testament, these are meant to support the memorization of the books. But don't spend so much time on the background that you run out of time for the activities.

The Big Thing

Bible Black Belts Pledge

Say the **Bible Black Belts Pledge** (page 15).

• Activity—Gospel, Gospel, Acts!

Supplies: Bibles

This game is a variation on Duck, Duck, Goose! Invite the children to sit on the floor in a circle. Pick one child to be "IT." This child will walk around the circle, lightly tapping each child on the head while saying the names of the different Gospels—Matthew, Mark, Luke, and John. When the child who is IT says, "Acts!" he or she tries to run all the way around the circle while the tagged child gives chase. If the IT child makes it all the way to the tagged child's spot and sits down, then the tagged child becomes the new IT. If the IT child gets caught and tagged, then he or she must remain IT for one more round.

This is the easy round. In Duck, Duck, Goose!, the children in the circle are listening closely to sounds of the words. What "goose" means or what "duck" means isn't important. But in this game, the children have to listen on two levels. First, they have to listen for five different possibilities. Second, they have to determine if what they heard is a Gospel or not. But within a few rounds, most children will know to simply listen for the word "Acts."

The next level of difficulty is to play this game using the Gospels and the Epistles (Letters). In this version, the IT child starts off by saying the names of different

Epistles. Then when he or she says the name of one of the Gospels, the chase is on. This is more difficult for a couple of reasons. First of all, there are many more names of books to consider now. Also, many of the Epistles, like all of the Gospels, are named after people. So the children have a lot more to think about.

One way to modify this game is by having the child who is IT try to escape by hopping around the circle on one leg. This will give the tagged child at least a chance.

Finally, you can include Acts and Revelation with the Gospels and Epistles, still having the children give chase when they hear the name of one of the four Gospels.

Consider creating a poster with all of the books of the New Testament (see page 40). Have the books divided into the four categories. The children can then refer to this poster as needed.

Also, we all have our own threshold when it comes to running in the classroom. You may choose to modify this game by always having the children hop around the circle rather than run. You can also modify this activity for a child who might have difficulty getting up to chase the IT child around the circle. For this child, perhaps the equivalent of running around the circle would be clapping eight times. If the child can clap eight times before the IT child makes it around the circle, then that counts as a tag.

• Activity—Sorting the Mail

Supplies: Bibles, card stock, assorted crayons

Maybe it's just me, but I've always had a much harder time memorizing the books of the New Testament than the Old Testament. And it's always the Epistles that trip me up. I can get Matthew, Mark, Luke, and John okay. And then Acts, and possibly Romans. But after that it's always a lot of mumbled confusion until Revelation. I think part of the confusion has to do with the seeming similarities of so many of the names—Philippians and Philemon, Corinthians and Colossians, John and Jude and James, and so forth.

The other contributing factor is that many of these are among the shortest, and therefore least visited, books of the Bible. I can recite you the entire Twenty-third Psalm before I can locate Philemon. (It's a whopping two pages long in the NRSV.) In fact, in the NRSV Children's Bible, the Book of Psalms is 104 pages, the exact same number of pages that contains the nineteen books from 2 Corinthians to Jude. These are some small (though not insignificant) books. That's why it's important to have an activity specifically to help children (and their teachers) navigate these less-familiar waters.

Supply the children with twenty-one sheets of card stock and assorted crayons. Have them put the name of a different Epistle on each sheet (see page 40). Make sure to have some extra sheets on hand, just in case. Allow the children to decorate the sheets by drawing postage stamps, as if these are envelopes going into the mail. Make sure the children know who is creating which Letter so that no Epistles get left out.

By the way, I like having the children create the letters rather than preparing them in advance. It gives the children one more way to connect to the material, this time by writing it.

Collect all the Letters and then shuffle them and redistribute them to the children. If you have fewer than twenty-one children in the room, some, if not all, the children will receive more than one Letter. If you have more than twenty-one children, you will simply need to take turns.

On your signal, have the children place the Letters on the floor from left to right in the order they occur in the Bible. If you like, you can have a poster in your room with all the books of the New Testament for the children to use as a reference. Better yet, if the kids get stumped, have them consult their Bibles or a classroom Bible.

Play this game many times.

• **For Reflection**
Ask: If you were going to write a letter telling someone else about the love of Jesus, what would you say?

Words of Celebration

Rejoice in the Lord always; again I will say, Rejoice.
Philippians 4:4

• Activity—Name Tag

Supplies: Bibles

Invite the children to sit with you on the floor in a circle. Have them pat their knees to a moderately slow steady beat. It's important to start slow and keep it slow. If you've ever been to a baseball game at a large stadium, you know that when the crowd starts clapping together, it inevitably speeds up and goes out of control.

As the children (and you) are patting, have them say the Scripture with you, in rhythm with the patting.

ReJOICE in the LORD Always; aGAIN I will SAY, reJOICE.

Once they are proficient at saying the Scripture in rhythm while patting, have them go back to just patting (still slowly).

You start the game by saying the Scripture in rhythm, followed immediately by the name of a child in the circle. For example:

ReJOICE in the LORD Always; aGAIN I will SAY, reJOICE. RaphaEL.

Raphael must immediately say the Scripture in rhythm, without missing a beat. (See why it's important to start slow?) After the Scripture, Raphael must call another child's name, and so on. Encourage the children to speak clearly and to make eye contact with the child whose name they are calling.

Facilitate play so that every child has a chance to say the Scripture and "tag" someone else by calling her or his name.

Once the children feel comfortable playing the game at the slow tempo, speed it up a bit. And be ready. The children love seeing if they can trip up their teachers.

• For Reflection

Ask: Have you ever done something that was so wonderful, you wanted to do it again right away? What is something in worship or Sunday school you would like to do again and again?

Words of Comfort

He will wipe every tear from their eyes. Death will be no more; mourning and crying and pain will be no more, for the first things have passed away.

Revelation 21:4

• Activity—Express Yourself

Supplies: Bibles

Divide the children into pairs. Have each pair find their own spot in the room. Have one child in each pair express an emotion using only facial expressions—no sounds, no body language. The other child must guess the emotion. Then have the partners switch roles.

Here is a short list of possible emotions to express:

Happy	Sad	Angry	Excited	Frightened
Confused	Lonely	Bored	Silly	Ecstatic

After each child in the pair has had a turn, have the children switch partners. I prefer to facilitate this myself, rather than have the children find partners on their own. Some children just seem to have plenty of kids wanting to be their partners, while others get left standing by themselves.

With the new partners, play Express Yourself again, this time using only body language—no sounds or facial expressions. After both children have had a turn, have the children switch partners again, reciting the Scripture aloud as they switch.

Next, play Express Yourself by reciting the Scripture. Have the children use only the sounds of their voices to express the emotions—no facial expressions or body language.

Some children may find this activity difficult, even frustrating. That doesn't mean you should avoid this activity in working with them, it simply means they will need additional help. One method that has proven successful is the use of emotion flash cards. These tend to be less subtle, and at least somewhat easier to read. Super Duper® Publications *(www.superduperinc.com)* has sets available. Do what works best for your setup, and most importantly, for the child.

• For Reflection

Ask: Think about a time you were very sad. Was anything or anyone able to cheer you up? (It's okay if the answer is no.) When have you helped someone who was sad feel better?

Words of Inspiration

You are the light of the world. A city on top of a hill can't be hidden. Neither do people light a lamp and put it under a basket. Instead, they put it on top of a lampstand, and it shines on all who are in the house. In the same way, let your light shine before people, so they can see the good things you do and praise your Father who is in heaven.
Matthew 5:14-16, CEB

• Activity—Basket/Light
Supplies: Bibles

This is a variation on the classic schoolyard game Red Light/Green Light.

Choose one child to be "IT." This child will stand against one wall while the other children line up against the opposite wall.

When the child who is IT calls out "Light," all the other children may head for the opposite wall. If you are uncomfortable having the children run inside (or if you have limited space in the room), consider having the children hop, hop on one foot, or walk like a lumbering animal such as an elephant. That will help extend the time it takes the children to get from one side of the room to the other. And it tends to be safer.

Anytime the child who is IT calls out "Basket," the other children must freeze. Those who don't freeze in time must go back to the wall and start over.

Here are a couple of variations of the game.

Turn out the lights and instead of having IT call out "Light" or "Basket," have this child hold a flashlight. When the flashlight is on, the children can move forward, and when the flashlight is off, the children must freeze. In this version, it is important for the children to not run. And it is super important to make sure the floor is clear of obstructions.

Another variation uses the spoken word. For this version, simply have the children stand in a circle. When the flashlight is on, the children start reciting the Scripture. When the light is off, the children must become silent. The first one to finish the Scripture wins. While this variation reinforces the Scripture in a more direct way, it will be harder to determine a winner. Make sure there are no children simply going, "Mumble-mumble-mumble-in heaven. I win!"

For this version, you may choose to have the Scripture posted on a wall. When the flashlight is on, it is directly pointed at the words. This will help the children since this Scripture is three verses long. As you play more and more rounds, have

the child who is IT simply turn the flashlight on and off, without pointing it at the posted Scripture.

If you can't find a flashlight or the batteries run down, simply use the room lights, with the child who is IT operating the switch. Allow each child the chance to be IT.

• For Reflection

Ask: What is something you do well that nobody knows about? How could you use that ability to glorify God?

Words of Wisdom

The fruit of the Spirit is love, joy, peace, patience, kindness,
goodness, faithfulness, gentleness, and self-control.

Galatians 5:22-23, CEB

• Activity—Fruit-of-the-Spirit Salad

Supplies: Bibles, card stock, markers or crayons

Give the children fifteen sheets of card stock and assorted markers or crayons.

Have nine children create pictures of the nine fruit of the Spirit. The pictures must include the word for each fruit of the Spirit.

Have six children make pictures of regular (edible) fruit, such as an apple, a banana, a bunch of grapes, and so on.

Once all the pictures have been made, take up all the cards.

Divide the children into two groups. One group will be the grocers, and the other group will be the shoppers.

Designate a portion of the room as the checkout line.

Have the shoppers close their eyes. Hand the cards to the grocers. The grocers are to spread the cards around the room, facing up, in as random an order as possible. They do not want to make things too easy for the shoppers. (Haven't you had that experience in a grocery store where everything seems to be in an unusual place, or they keep moving things? It's almost as if they want you to stay in the store as long as possible.)

Then invite the shoppers to open their eyes. They are shopping for the ingredients for fruit-of-the-Spirit salad. They need all nine items, without any of the other fruits. The shoppers can work as a team finding all the different fruit-of-the-Spirit cards.

When the shoppers get all nine items to the checkout line, they must arrange them in the same order as they appear in the Scripture, otherwise—no sale!

Once they have done this, have the children switch roles and play again.

You can add an interesting wrinkle by having the other six fruits be other fine attributes, just not those mentioned in the Scripture passage. Some examples are tolerance, hospitality, honesty, humility, prayerfulness, and dependability.

This will make it trickier for the shoppers.

Play this game several times, and see how fast the children can go.

• For Reflection

Ask: Which ingredient in fruit-of-the-Spirit salad is your favorite? Why?

Words of Jesus

This is my commandment, that you love one another
as I have loved you.

John 15:12

• Activity—Stomp

Supplies: Bibles

This is a very simple and recognizable activity for anyone who has ever attended a college or professional football, basketball, soccer, hockey, or baseball game in America.

It's based on that STOMP-STOMP-CLAP rhythm the crowd does to get things "revved up." In this case, we will simply add a verse of Scripture to the mix.

Have the children stand with you and start the STOMP-STOMP-CLAP rhythm. Then add the Scripture as you continue the rhythm.

This   is   my com-   mand- ment, that you
STOMP STOMP CLAP   STOMP STOMP CLAP

love   one an- oth-   er as
STOMP STOMP CLAP   STOMP STOMP CLAP

I   have   loved
STOMP STOMP CLAP   STOMP STOMP CLAP

you.
STOMP STOMP CLAP   STOMP STOMP CLAP

Do this several times. Get softer. Get louder. Use a high voice. Use a deep voice. Find ways to add repetitions without making it feel repetitive.

• For Reflection

Ask: Do you think we can really love one another as Jesus loves us? What things could make that tricky for us?

This is my commandment, that you love one another as I have loved you.

John 15:12

Green Belt Level

The Big Thing: Bible Black Belts Pledge, The Peaceable Kingdom (Isaiah 11:6-9)

Words of Celebration: Luke 1:46-47

Words of Comfort: Luke 2:10-11, KJV

Words of Inspiration: John 3:16, CEB

Words of Wisdom: Proverbs 20:11

Words of Jesus: Matthew 19:14

The Peaceable Kingdom

The wolf will live with the lamb,
the leopard will lie down with the goat,
the calf and the lion and the yearling together;
and a little child will lead them.

The cow will feed with the bear,
their young will lie down together,
and the lion will eat straw like the ox.

The infant will play near the hole of the cobra,
and the young child put his hand into the viper's nest.

They will neither harm nor destroy
on all my holy mountain,
for the earth will be full of the knowledge of the LORD
as the waters cover the sea.

(Isaiah 11:6-9, NIV)

I prefer the New International Version for this passage. The activities that follow are drama-based, which makes the NRSV a little tricky. With the NIV, I don't have to worry about which child to cast as the "fatling" or how children will demonstrate the difference between the "nursing child" and the "weaned child."

The Big Thing

Bible Black Belts Pledge

Say the **Bible Black Belts Pledge** (page 15).

• Activity—A Child Shall Lead Them

Supplies: Bibles, index cards, markers

Before the session, prepare eighteen index cards, each with one of the animals or people from the Scripture.

Wolf	Lamb
Leopard	Goat
Calf	Lion
Yearling (year-old cow)	Little child will lead them
Cow	Bear
Young cow	Young bear
Lion	Ox
Infant	Cobra
Young child	Viper

Speak through the Scripture several times. Consider having it posted on a wall so that all the children can see it.

Hand each child a card. There are eighteen cards in all. If you have fewer than eighteen children, then pull out a few cards. Make sure to pull out the groupings, such as wolf/lamb or infant/cobra, so that there are no incomplete pairs among the cards you hand out.

Make sure the cards that are not handed out are laid out on the floor, facing up, so that the names on each card are clearly visible.

The child with the card reading "Little child will lead them" is "IT."

The other children must hold their cards so that IT can read them.

The child who is IT must rearrange the children so that they are standing in Scripture order based on their cards. With a smaller group, the child who is IT can also take the cards that are on the floor and arrange them among the children, so that all the animals and people are accounted for.

Once IT has arranged all the children, have the entire group recite the Scripture to check the work.

Here is a more challenging, and more fun, version of the game. Hand out the cards as before, but this time, make sure the children do not show their cards to anyone else.

They must use pantomime and sound effects to demonstrate the animal or person on their cards.

This will be tricky, considering there are many similarities among these animals and people, such as the lamb and goat, the lion and the leopard, the infant and the young child, the cobra and the viper. Challenge the children to find any characteristic, visual or vocal, that will allow their animal or person to be distinguished from all others. You may even want to agree, as a group, on what the distinguishing characteristics of each animal and person are before playing.

The child who is IT must arrange the children in Scripture order, based on the sights and sounds. Once IT has all the children arranged, have the entire group recite the Scripture to check the order. With this version, there might be some mistakes: "Oh. You're the calf. I thought you were the yearling." Allow the child who is IT to make adjustments, then have the group recite the Scripture one more time.

While it would be great to allow each child to be IT, the reality is that this game takes a little more time than some of the others. By the time you've played it three or four times, the children will be ready to move on.

• For Reflection
Ask: How does it feel when those around you get along? How does it feel when they don't get along?

Words of Celebration

My soul magnifies the Lord, and my spirit rejoices in God my Savior.

Luke 1:46-47

• Activity—Growing

Supplies: Bibles

Invite the children to each find some open space on the floor and sit down. Have the children roll up tightly into balls on the floor and softly recite the Scripture. Have them continue to repeat the Scripture as they open up and get gradually louder.

Next, have them continue reciting the Scripture a little more loudly as they stand up. Then have them spread their arms out wide as they continue.

Finally, have them stretch way up high, fingers spread wide as they loudly proclaim the Scripture.

• For Reflection

Ask: Have you ever felt very small compared to all those who were around you? Are there times when you hope the power of God's love can make you feel bigger than you really are?

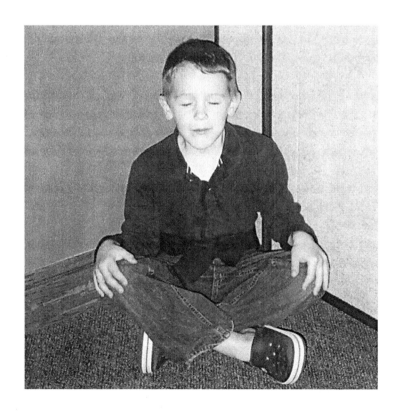

Words of Comfort

*And the angel said unto them, Fear not: for, behold, I bring you good tidings of
great joy, which shall be to all people. For unto you is born this day
in the city of David a Saviour, which is Christ the Lord.*

Luke 2:10-11, KJV

• Activity—Fear-Not Freeze Tag

Supplies: Bibles

People back in Bible times must have been more skittish, or angels must have been
pretty scary looking. Because it seems like every time in the Bible an angel appears to
someone, the first thing the angel has to say is, "Fear not" or "Be not afraid."

Start by having the children sit with you in a circle on the floor. Recite the Scripture.
Most of the children have at least heard this Scripture before. You can ask:

- Who is the angel speaking to? *(the shepherds)*
- What is the name of the Savior? *(Jesus)*
- Where will they find the baby? *(in a manger)*

Have the children recite the Scripture a few times. Then have all the children stand up.
Choose one child to be "IT."

The other children can move about the room, walking, hopping, skipping, walking
backwards, moving like jungle animals, pretending to play sports, and so on. As they are
moving, they must recite the Scripture aloud in unison.

At any point, the child who is IT can call out "Freeze!" and all the children must stop
reciting and freeze in whatever positions they find themselves in at that exact moment.
When IT wants the children to unfreeze, he or she simply says, "Fear not." At that point,
the children continue moving and reciting the Scripture wherever they left off.

After a short time, choose a new child to be IT. Allow each child a chance to be IT.

• For Reflection

Ask: Have you ever been scared of a grownup you have just met, but then found out that
grownup was a very nice person?

Words of Inspiration

For God so loved the world that he gave his only Son,
so that everyone who believes in him won't perish but will have eternal life.

John 3:16, CEB

• Activity—Add a Word
Supplies: Bibles

This is a simple yet effective game for aiding memorization.

Have the children sit with you in a circle on the floor.

Choose one child to start by saying the first word of the Scripture.

The child immediately to her or his right must say the first and second words.

Continue adding words child-by-child, until the Scripture is spoken by one child in its entirety.

Child 1: *For*
Child 2: *For God*
Child 3: *For God so*
Child 4: *For God so loved*

And so on.

This activity can work well with many different Scriptures. It is best, however, to use it with short passages. Even John 3:16, which seems very short, still has 26 words according to the CEB.

Make sure the children in the circle give the one who is speaking a chance to think of the next word to add. Sometimes well-meaning children will try to help by saying the answer for someone else, when all that may be needed is a few extra seconds.

• For Reflection
Ask: Have you ever loved someone so much that you gave something to that person that meant a great deal to you? What did you give?

Words of Wisdom

Even children make themselves known by their acts,
by whether what they do is pure and right.

Proverbs 20:11

• Activity—The Puppet Pupil

Supplies: Bibles, one hand puppet

Have the children speak through the Scripture a few times.

It is possible that after only a few times, many of the children will have the Scripture committed to memory. But many, while they have the basic gist, may still be struggling a bit with the exact wording.

Bring out the hand puppet. You can give it a name, a special voice, a persona, whatever you wish.

The puppet can say something like, "Hello, kiddos! I couldn't help overhearing that you are learning a Bible verse. I want to learn it too. Let's play a game. How about you be the teachers and I'll be the student. I'll try to say the Scripture, and you let me know when I mess up. Let's give it a go."

Children love this activity. They will listen attentively as the puppet starts reciting the Scripture. But along the way, the puppet will say the wrong word and the children will most likely laugh and then offer the correct word to the puppet. Encourage the children to be gentle with their corrections.

Example:

Puppet: Even chickens make . . .

Children: *{laughter}* No, it's not "chickens," it's "children."

Puppet: Oh, my mistake. Okay. Let's try that again. Even children make themselves purple by . . .

Children: *{more laughter}* It's not "make themselves purple," it's "make themselves known."

Puppet: Oh. Yes, that makes more sense. You're very good teachers. Let's try it again.

Always start at the beginning. Have each subsequent mistake be a little further along in the Scripture until the puppet finally makes it through. This is usually met with applause from the children.

Now, have the puppet and the children all join in reciting the Scripture together.

This activity works for several reasons. First of all, the children are being led by someone besides you (sort of). Don't be surprised if you become completely invisible as the children, even the older ones, talk directly to the puppet. Second, the children are listening critically throughout. Third, they are hearing the Scripture many, many times. But because they are so focused on being the teachers, they hardly notice that they are being taught.

By the way, don't worry about your puppetry technique. Kids have amazing imaginations. You can stand right in front of them, holding the puppet, with your mouth moving right there in plain sight, and it won't faze the kids one bit. And don't worry too much about the age of the children. I've found that people of all ages find puppetry engaging. As long as you aren't talking down to the kids or trying to make your voice too goofy, they'll play along.

And this activity can work for virtually any Bible verse. Also, consider having a few more puppets in the room. Divide the children into groups of three or four, and let them each take turns using the puppets to do the activity.

• For Reflection
Ask: What is something you can do this very day that will glorify God and inspire others?

Words of Jesus

*Jesus said, "Let the little children come to me, and do not stop them;
for it is to such as these that the kingdom of heaven belongs."*

Matthew 19:14

• Activity—Obstacle Course

*Supplies: Bibles; various objects, such as masking tape, a few lengths of yarn, and clean empty
plastic soda bottles*

Divide the children into two groups.

Have one group go to a corner of the room with you to practice reciting the Scripture.

Give the other group various objects such as masking tape, a few lengths of yarn, and
empty plastic soda bottles (clean, please).

These children are to use the objects to make an obstacle course around the room.

Tape can be used to make a start and finish line or a balance beam. Yarn can be used to
make a moderate gap to jump across or a winding path. Soda bottles can serve as hazard
cones to weave in and out of. The only limitations are the imagination of the children and
a safety check by you. No jumping over yarn "high-jump" bars. Going under is just fine.

Once the obstacle course has been created by one group, the other children must run the
course one at a time. As one child is running the course, all the children from her or his
group are to recite the Scripture to "cheer on" that child.

Allow each child who did not set up the obstacle course to run it.

Then have the groups switch roles, so that one group works on the Scripture with you
while the other group gets to create a new obstacle course.

• For Reflection

Ask: Have you ever felt disappointed that you weren't allowed to do something because
you were "just a kid"? How does it feel to know that in God's eyes, you are just as
precious as anyone else in the world—even the President of the United States?

Jesus said, "Let the little children come to me, and do not stop them; for it is to such as these that the kingdom of heaven belongs."

Matthew 19:14

Blue Belt Level

The Big Thing: Bible Black Belts Pledge, The Ten Commandments (Exodus 20:2-17)

Words of Celebration: Psalm 95:1

Words of Comfort: Isaiah 40:31

Words of Inspiration: 2 Corinthians 3:17

Words of Wisdom: Colossians 3:20-21, CEB

Words of Jesus: Luke 10:27

The Ten Commandments
Based on Exodus 20:2-17

I am the Lord Your God.

1. You shall have no gods before me.

2. You shall not make and worship idols.

3. You shall not misuse my name.

4. You shall remember the sabbath day, and keep it holy.

5. Honor your father and mother.

6. You shall not kill.

7. You shall not commit adultery.

8. You shall not steal.

9. You shall not tell lies about others.

10. You shall not want things that belong to others.

I just had to go with a paraphrase here. I've got one hour with the kids each week, if I'm lucky. That's just enough time to teach "Remember the sabbath day, and keep it holy." The full version, "Remember the sabbath day, and keep it holy. Six days you shall labor and do all your work. But the seventh day is a sabbath to the LORD your God; you shall not do any work—you, your son or your daughter, your male or female slave, your livestock, or the alien resident in your towns.

For in six days the L<small>ORD</small> made heaven and earth, the sea, and all that is in them, but rested the seventh day; therefore the L<small>ORD</small> blessed the sabbath day and consecrated it," would take the better part of a month, leaving us nine more commandments to go.

Some questions from the kids:

"What's a sabbath?" (*The word* sabbath *means "to cease." It is to be a day set aside to rest and worship God.*)

"What does *covet* mean?" (*To* covet *means to want something that belongs to someone else.*)

"What is adultery?" You might as well get ready. This question is coming. We all have our own comfort level, or discomfort level, with regard to teaching what adultery is. I can't tell you the most appropriate response for your setting. Here is what I choose to say: *When two people get married, they promise to love each other and be faithful to one another. That means they promise not to fall in love with someone else. Adultery means falling in love with someone who is not your spouse.* Is this the 100% whole story about adultery? No. Is this as thoroughly as I feel comfortable explaining it with a room full of children who all come from different households where vastly different parenting philosophies are in place? Absolutely!

The Big Thing

Bible Black Belts Pledge
Say the **Bible Black Belts Pledge** (page 15).

• Activity—Rules
Supplies: Bibles, posterboard (pre-numbered 1-10), markers, card stock

Have the children stand.

Say: Okay, let's play a game. Ready … go! (Most likely, the children will just look at you blankly. Others may make some manic motions with no real direction.) Hmm, that didn't go like I'd hoped. Maybe we need a rule, just one. I've got it! The rule will be—everyone do exactly what I say to do.

Say: Hop three times. ➜ Stop hopping.
Run in place. ➜ Stop running.
Raise your right arm ➜ Lower your right arm.
Raise your left arm. ➜ Lower your left arm.

Say: Well that wasn't any better than the first way. You're just doing whatever I tell you to do. That's not a very fun game. I think we need another rule. How about this—whenever I start by saying, "Simon Says," then do whatever I say after that. But if I don't start with "Simon Says," then do not do what I say after that.

Lead the children through a game of Simon Says for a few minutes.

Say: See? We just needed a few rules. Rules can be important and God gave us ten really important ones. What are those rules called? *(Children will respond, "The Ten Commandments!")* That's right. How many of the Ten Commandments can we come up with as a class?

Use a piece of posterboard pre-numbered 1-10 and a marker to jot down the correct answers. Put the answers in their correct slot according to the Scripture. For example, if a child calls out, "You shall not kill," put that next to the number 6.

If the children as a group get all ten, awesome! If, however, there are some blanks, invite the children to find the Ten Commandments in Exodus 20:2-17. Allow the children to call out the remaining commandments to fill in the blanks.

Give each child two pieces of card stock and a marker. Have each child write the Ten Commandments on the sheets of card stock without numbering them.

The children may also decorate the card stock to look like tablets.

Once every child has created her or his Ten Commandments, give the children scissors and instruct them to cut their card stock into ten pieces, with one commandment on each piece.

Then have them mix up the pieces and put them back together.

• For Reflection
Ask: What rule, at school or at home, is the most difficult for you to follow? If you could add an eleventh commandment, what would it be?

Bible Black Belts

Words of Celebration

O come, let us sing to the Lord;
let us make a joyful noise to the rock of our salvation!
Psalm 95:1

• Activity—Joyful Noises
Supplies: Bibles

Have the children sit on the floor in a circle. Say the Scripture aloud with them a few times.

Choose one child to close her or his eyes.

Next, silently select another child to say the Scripture aloud.

Now, here's the catch. That child must use a high voice, low voice, nasal voice, silly voice, husky voice, or any other possible kind of voice to disguise her or his natural speaking voice.

The child whose eyes are closed must listen. Then the child can open her or his eyes and try to guess who recited the Scripture.

Allow each child a chance to recite the Scripture using a different voice.

• For Reflection
Ask: What's the most joyful noise you've ever heard? What's the most joyful noise you've ever made?

Words of Comfort

But those who wait for the LORD shall renew their strength,
they shall mount up with wings like eagles,
they shall run and not be weary, they shall walk and not faint.

Isaiah 40:31

• Activity—Embody Scripture
Supplies: Bibles

Invite the children to sit with you in a circle. Read the Scripture aloud. Next, have the children spread out on the floor and guide them through actions that embody the Scripture.

Here is a simple process to follow:
1. Say each part by itself.
2. Say each part and add the corresponding motion.
3. Say and do all five in order.
4. Perform the motions without speaking the text.

Those who wait for the LORD — *Lie on your back with your hands folded over your chest.*
Shall renew their strength — *Sit up and flex your muscles.*
They shall mount up with wings like eagles — *Stand and flap your arms like they are wings.*
They shall run and not be weary — *Run in place.*
They shall walk and not faint — *Walk in place.*

Once the children can do all the motions in the correct sequence without hearing or reciting the Scripture, play another game.

Have the children sit in a circle on the floor. Invite a child to perform one of the five motions that corresponds to a line of Scripture. The other children must guess what part of the Scripture is being performed. If time permits, give each child a turn.

As a wrap-up, have the children all recite the entire Scripture as they perform the motions. Then challenge them to recite the Scripture without performing the motions.

• For Reflection
Ask: Have you ever felt weighed down with too many chores, never-ending homework, or any other responsibilities? How could faith in the power of God help get you through those times?

Words of Inspiration

Now the Lord is the Spirit, and
where the Spirit of the Lord is, there is freedom.

2 Corinthians 3:17

• Activity—Signing the Scripture

Supplies: Bibles

Sign language can be a very effective way to internalize Scripture. Aside from being a vital means of communication for millions of people, sign language is a highly expressive language. There have been times when seeing a passage of Scripture signed has helped me find a deeper understanding of that passage. And it gives children a chance to do more than hear Scripture. Sign language broadens the senses and allows us to see and to do.

Teach the children the signs for *Lord, Spirit*, and *freedom*. Two helpful websites I turn to are *http://aslbrowser.commtechlab.msu.edu/browser.htm* and *www.aslpro.com*. Both sites have video dictionaries that demonstrate how to sign the words. As of the publication of this resource, both sites were up and running.

Once the children have learned the signs, have them incorporate the signs into the Scripture as they recite it aloud. Next, have them think the verse and sign at the appropriate times without speaking the Scripture aloud.

Incidentally, there are signs for the other words in the Scripture, but learning these few signs for the keywords will help with memorization and will give the signing a better sense of flow.

• For Reflection

Ask: If you could have one more hour of free time each week, what would you do?

Words of Wisdom

Children, obey your parents in everything,
because this pleases the Lord. Parents, don't provoke your children
in a way that ends up discouraging them.

Colossians 3:20-21, CEB

• Activity—Mama Says/Papa Says
Supplies: Bibles, posterboard, marker

As you might imagine, when I asked several parents to submit favorite Bible verses to consider for *Bible Black Belts,* many of them sent me "Honor your father and your mother" (Exodus 20:12).

Interestingly, no one suggested this passage from Colossians. This is one of my favorite passages of Scripture, maybe because I've always questioned authority. It has a certain balance to it. Yes, children, we want you to honor your parents. But we parents have a responsibility to treat our children in such a way that we merit that honor. Shared responsibility—LOVE it!

This game is a variation on Simon Says.

Ask the children to come up with pleasing things to do (or ways to behave). Write these down on a large piece of posterboard titled "Pleasing," and place it on a wall where all can see.

Next, ask the children to come up with a list of unacceptable things to do. Write these down on a large piece of posterboard titled "Not Pleasing," and place it on the wall next to the other poster.

Here is a sample list for each.

Pleasing
1. Make your bed.
2. Put dishes in the sink.
3. Brush your teeth.
4. Eat your veggies.
5. Read your library book.
6. Help your little brother tie his shoes.
7. Say your prayers.
8. Put a quarter in the church collection plate.
9. Scratch your dog behind her ears.
10. Play catch with your best friend.

Not Pleasing

1. Eat ten cookies at one time.
2. Push your sister down.
3. Turn away from a friend in need.
4. Put spaghetti on your head.
5. Laugh when someone else gets hurt.
6. Jump on your bed.
7. Throw your dirty clothes on the floor.

Have all the children stand up. Choose one child to be the Mama or Papa. This child then tells the others what to do, choosing from the Pleasing or Not Pleasing list. The child also starts every command with "Mama says" or "Papa says."

For example: Mama says brush your teeth. If the command is from the Pleasing list, then the children obey it by pantomiming the actions of that acceptable task. If the command comes from the Not Pleasing list, the children must stand very still and wait for the next command.

Remind the children that they aren't listening for whether or not the command begins with "Mama says" or "Papa says." They are listening to see whether or not the command is something they should do.

Allow each child a chance to be Mama or Papa. Every time you switch to a new Mama or Papa, have the entire group recite the Scripture.

By the way, you may need to clarify—this activity is not about giving children the go-ahead to disobey their parents. Yes, children, it is important to obey your parents. And the reason it is okay to do so is because your parents care about you very much and want you to get the most out of life.

• For Reflection

Ask: Has anyone ever tried to get you to do something you knew wasn't right? If you were in charge, would you try to make somebody do something from the Not Pleasing list?

Words of Jesus

You shall love the Lord your God with all your heart, and with all your soul, and with all your strength, and with all your mind; and your neighbor as yourself.

Luke 10:27

• Activity—Embodying Scripture
Supplies: Bibles

Teach the children a different motion to perform as they recite each part of the Scripture.

> **You shall love the Lord your God** — *Point out with the index fingers of both hands.*
> **With all your heart** — *Put your hands over your heart.*
> **And with all your soul** — *Make your arms move in arching circles over your head (or consult www.aslpro.com or http://aslbrowser.commtechlab.msu.edu/browser.htm for the sign for "soul").*
> **And with all your strength** — *Flex your muscles.*
> **And with all your mind** — *Point to your brain with both hands.*
> **And your neighbor as yourself** — *Clasp your hands together in front, then pull them in toward your chest.*

Once the children have learned all the motions, challenge them to perform the motions silently while thinking the Scripture.

As a fun follow-up activity, select a child to perform one of the motions. The others must say the portion of Scripture that corresponds with the motion. If there is enough time, allow each child the chance to act out a portion of the Scripture.

Embodying Scripture is a wonderful, simple, and expressive activity that can work for many different passages of Scripture. The trick is to make the motions distinct for each passage, so that those motions are specifically associated with the text.

• For Reflection
Ask: This passage of Scripture from Luke 10:27 is based on the "Shema" found in Deuteronomy 6:5. People have been memorizing Scripture for a long time. What is your favorite Scripture that you've learned so far?

You shall love
the Lord your God
with all your heart,
and with all your soul,
and with all your
strength,
and with all your mind;
and your neighbor as
yourself.

Luke 10:27

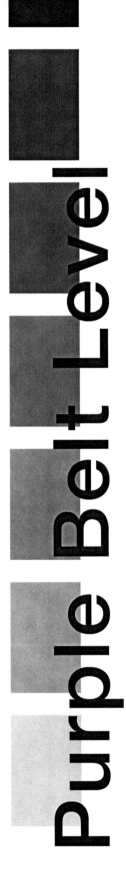

Purple Belt Level

The Big Thing: Bible Black Belts Pledge, The Twenty-third Psalm

Words of Celebration: Psalm 107:1

Words of Comfort: Joshua 1:9

Words of Inspiration: Philippians 4:13

Words of Wisdom: Proverbs 21:3

Words of Jesus: John 12:26, CEB

Psalm 23

1. The LORD is my shepherd; I shall not want.

2. He maketh me to lie down in green pastures:
   he leadeth me beside the still waters.

3. He restoreth my soul: he leadeth me in the paths
   of righteousness for his name's sake.

4. Yea, though I walk through the valley of the shadow of death,
   I will fear no evil: for thou art with me;
   thy rod and thy staff they comfort me.

5. Thou preparest a table before me in the presence of mine enemies:
   thou anointest my head with oil; my cup runneth over.

6. Surely goodness and mercy shall follow me all the days of my life:
   and I will dwell in the house of the LORD for ever.

(King James Version)

There's no getting around it. When it comes to the Twenty-third Psalm, the King James Version is a favorite. For some it's the sense of tradition, for some it's the sheer beauty of the language, and for others it's deeply sentimental. Most of us have attended many funerals and memorial services for loved ones where the King James Version of Psalm 23 was read. While I appreciate new translations and modern language, when it comes to Psalm 23, I find myself drawn to the KJV.

The Big Thing

Bible Black Belts Pledge

Say the **Bible Black Belts Pledge** (page 15).

• Activity—Scripture Journey

Supplies: Bibles; construction paper; long sheets of butcher paper; assorted crayons or markers; found objects such as plastic soda bottles, cardboard tubes, and cardboard boxes; scissors; tape

Aside from being one of the most beloved passages of Scripture in the entire Bible, and even one of the great works of literature, it is a *Bible Black Belts* teacher's dream. There is plenty of action and descriptive language. Each of the six verses has its own identity. And yet the whole holds together, almost like a good story.

For this activity, provide construction paper; long sheets of butcher paper; assorted crayons or markers; found objects such as plastic soda bottles, cardboard tubes, and cardboard boxes; scissors; and tape.

Divide the children into six groups, and have each group go to an open space in the room.

Assign each group to set the scene for one of the six verses of Psalm 23.

Invite the children to use the materials you have provided (remind them to share) to help them set the scene for their verse. Encourage the children in each group to come up with a plan before diving headfirst into the materials.

Allow several minutes for this.

Once each group has finished setting the scene for their verse, have each group present their scene to the others. Then recite the entire psalm, with Group 1 reciting the first verse from within their scene, Group 2 reciting the second verse, and so on.

By this point, each group should be pretty familiar with their own verse. Now we want all the children to be able to put the verses together. Take the children on a Scripture journey. Start in the setting for verse 1, created by Group 1, and have the children recite that verse. Then move on to the setting for the second verse. Continue until all the children have journeyed through all six settings and spoken all six verses. It may be necessary to take a few small groups on separate journeys, rather than all the children at one time.

Along the journey, invite the children to use their imaginations in connection with their senses. For example, in the setting for verse 2, you may ask them to imagine hearing the breeze blowing through the grass, or to imagine dipping their hands into the cool, refreshing water. For verse 5, you could invite them to imagine the smells of the wonderful food at the table.

As a final step, have the children find an open place on the floor to lie down. Next, invite them to recite the Psalm 23 Scripture in unison softly as they imagine their own Scripture journeys.

• For Reflection
Ask: In the whole Bible, which Scripture helps you most to feel comforted? Can you think of a time when the Twenty-third Psalm might help you feel comforted?

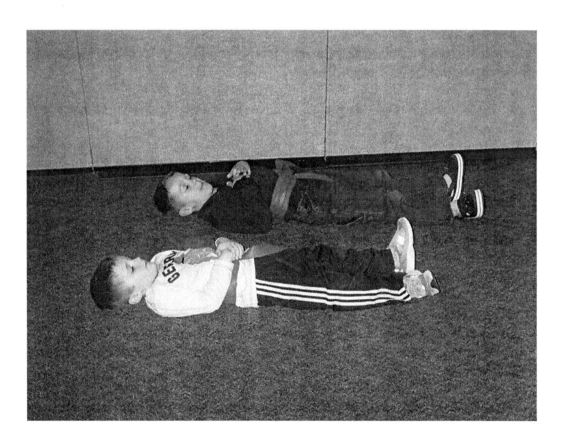

Words of Celebration

O give thanks to the LORD, for he is good;
for his steadfast love endures forever.

Psalm 107:1

• Activity—Infinity Walk

Supplies: Bibles, paper, marker, masking tape

This is an activity I learned from my good friend Barbara Bruce during one of her famous brain breaks. Not only will this activity help reinforce the Scripture, but it has wonderful brain benefits. The Infinity Walk stimulates the brain by involving both hemispheres, and makes a great activity throughout the year. The symbol for *infinity* is much like a figure eight on its side.

Make sure you have plenty of open space in the room. Use tape to mark two spots on the floor, approximately four feet apart. If space allows, set up more than one infinity "course."

Have the children walk around the spots, crossing through the middle so that they are walking in a figure-eight (infinity) pattern.

Then have the children swing their arms as they walk—right arm with left foot, left arm with right foot.

Next, invite the children to recite Psalm 107:1 aloud as they walk.

Finally, post a sheet of paper on a wall reading, "God's steadfast loves endures forever." Have the children focus on the sign as they walk the infinity pattern.

It will most likely be necessary to have one child at a time on each infinity course. This will keep the kiddos from bumping into each other as they focus on the sign (not to mention it will keep them from crashing into each other as they inevitably meet in the middle).

• For Reflection

Ask: What was the longest time you've ever spent on one activity? (The longest time you've spent in the swimming pool. The longest time you've ever slept.) Can you imagine doing the same thing forever?

Words of Comfort

I hereby command you: Be strong and courageous;
do not be frightened or dismayed,
for the LORD your God is with you wherever you go.

Joshua 1:9

• Activity—Mirror Game

Supplies: Bibles

Divide the children into pairs. Have the children in each pair stand about three feet apart, facing one another. One child in each pair must move very slowly, using hands, arms, legs, head, and facial expressions. The other child must try to mirror those motions as exactly as possible. The whole time they do this, they must recite the Scripture. Once they have recited the Scripture twice, the pairs much switch roles and play again.

It is important to make the movements slow and deliberate. The object isn't to trick the other person, but for both partners to stay together and move in sync.

• For Reflection

Ask: When was the last time you were really scared? Did it help knowing that God was right there with you?

Words of Inspiration

I can do all things through {Christ} who strengthens me.
Philippians 4:13

• Activity—Body Percussion
Supplies: Bibles

This Scripture will be spoken accompanied by body percussion. Have the children stand with you in a circle, and teach them the body percussion pattern. It's very simple.

Stomp-stomp   pat-pat *(pat thighs)*   clap-clap   flex muscles

Have the children do this with you several times in a row until they are comfortable with the pattern. Next, introduce the Scripture. It corresponds with the body percussion like this:

I can do all   **things through**   **Christ who**   **strength**ens me.
Stomp stomp   pat   pat   clap clap   flex

Have the children join you in reciting the Scripture several times while performing the body percussion.

Now add a new wrinkle to the activity. Start by having the children say the Scripture as they perform the body percussion. Then have them do only the body percussion. Repeat these steps multiple times.

There are a couple of benefits to alternating the Scripture accompanied by body percussion with the body percussion alone. First of all, it helps make the repetitions of the Scripture seem a little less repetitive. Second, it helps the children internalize the Scripture. At first, when the children are performing the body percussion by itself, they will most likely be thinking, "Stomp-stomp pat-pat clap-clap flex." But as they get more comfortable with the rhythm, they will start to internalize the text—think it without having to say it out loud. This is an important memorization step.

• For Reflection
Ask: What does it mean to be able to do all things through Christ? Does that mean we can do anything we want, just because we want to do it? Is there a difference between being able to do what we want to do and what God wants us to do? Have you ever felt that Christ gave you the strength you needed to do something meaningful?

Words of Wisdom

To do righteousness and justice is more acceptable to the LORD than sacrifice.
Proverbs 21:3

• Activity—Balance Beam
Supplies: Bibles, masking tape

The purpose of this activity is to help build an understanding that Lent doesn't always have to be about sacrifice or giving up something we really like. We maintain balance when we add something new that enriches our spiritual journey.

Use tape to make a long, straight line on the floor. This will be the balance beam.

Have the children stand and recite the Scripture with you a few times.

Next have the children line up at one end of the balance beam.

Have the children walk the beam as they recite the Scripture.

You can repeat this activity a few times.

For a variation of this activity, challenge the children to walk the balance beam without looking down. They can pick a spot on the wall and focus as they walk and say the Scripture. Then at the end, the children can look down and see how they did.

• For Reflection
Ask: Have you or someone you know ever given up anything for Lent? (for instance, given up chocolate, given up watching TV) Have you or someone you know ever taken on anything new during Lent? (for example, started journaling, started eating one more green vegetable each day, started calling your grandmother more often)

Words of Jesus

Whoever serves me must follow me. Wherever I am, there my servant will also be. My Father will honor whoever serves me.

John 12:26, CEB

• Activity—Follow the Leader
Supplies: Bibles

Given the Scripture, Follow the Leader makes the ideal game to reinforce the message. Nothing fancy here. Choose one child to serve as the leader. This child can walk, skip, hop, wave arms, make any motions he or she wants (provided they are safe and not overwhelmingly gross). The others must follow as exactly as possible.

Here's the one wrinkle—the children must do all this while reciting John 12:26. After several seconds, switch to a new leader. Allow each child an opportunity to lead the others.

This is another one of those games where it's very important to have a lot of clear, open space. Eliminate all the hard edges and sharp corners you can.

• For Reflection
Ask: Think of a time when you trusted someone enough that you followed that person without knowing for sure where you were going.

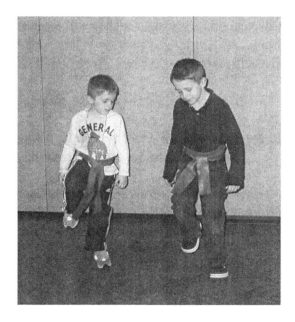

Red Belt Level

The Big Thing: Bible Black Belts Pledge, The Beatitudes (Matthew 5:3-12)

Words of Celebration: Isaiah 9:2

Words of Comfort: Matthew 11:28

Words of Inspiration: 1 John 4:12

Words of Wisdom: Proverbs 14:31

Words of Jesus: Matthew 5:45

The Beatitudes

Blessed are the poor in spirit, for theirs is the kingdom of heaven.

Blessed are those who mourn, for they will be comforted.

Blessed are the meek, for they will inherit the earth.

Blessed are those who hunger and thirst for righteousness,
for they will be filled.

Blessed are the merciful, for they will receive mercy.

Blessed are the pure in heart, for they will see God.

Blessed are the peacemakers, for they will be called children of God.

Blessed are those who are persecuted for righteousness' sake,
for theirs is the kingdom of heaven.

Blessed are you when people revile you and persecute you and utter all kinds of evil
against you falsely on my account. Rejoice and be glad, for your reward is great in
heaven, for in the same way they persecuted the prophets
who were before you.

(Matthew 5:3-12)

The Big Thing

Bible Black Belts Pledge
Say the **Bible Black Belts Pledge** (page 15).

• Activity—Beatitude Buddies
Supplies: Bibles, index cards (same color and size), pencils

Divide the children into pairs. Give each child an index card and a pencil.

For this activity, make sure all the index cards are the same color and size.

Assign a different beatitude to each pair. You will need nine pairs of children in all. Otherwise, some pairs may have to do a little extra. Have one child in each pair write the first part of the beatitude on one card and the other child write the second part on the other card.

Make sure the children write legibly.

Pair 1
1st Card — Blessed are the poor in spirit,
2nd Card — for theirs is the kingdom of heaven.

Pair 2
1st Card — Blessed are those who mourn,
2nd Card — for they will be comforted.

Pair 3
1st Card — Blessed are the meek,
2nd Card — for they will inherit the earth.

Pair 4
1st Card — Blessed are those who hunger and thirst for
          righteousness,
2nd Card — for they will be filled.

Pair 5
1st Card — Blessed are the merciful,
2nd Card — for they will receive mercy.

Pair 6
1st Card — Blessed are the pure in heart,
2nd Card — for they will see God.

Pair 7
1st Card — Blessed are the peacemakers,
2nd Card — for they will be called children of God.

Pair 8
1st Card — Blessed are those who are persecuted for righteousness' sake,
2nd Card — for theirs is the kingdom of heaven.

Pair 9
1st Card — Blessed are you when people revile you and persecute you and utter all kinds of evil against you falsely on my account.
2nd Card — Rejoice and be glad, for your reward is great in heaven, for in the same way they persecuted the prophets who were before you.

Notice a couple of things. First, Pair 9 has by far the longest of the Beatitudes. It really has a different rhythm and flow than any of the other eight. Second, in pairs 1 and 8 the second card is identical.

Once all the children have finished creating the cards, take them up, along with the pencils and any extra cards floating around.

Read Matthew 5:3-12 aloud.

Next, shuffle all the cards and redistribute them to the children.

Have the children stand and start saying aloud the portion of the Scripture that is on their individual cards. This will sound pretty cacophonic. The children must walk around the room, saying their part of the beatitude and listening for the child who is saying the other part of that same beatitude. They are searching for their Beatitude Buddies. Once all the children have found their buddies, have each pair say the entire beatitude for the others. You may choose to have the Beatitudes posted on a wall where the children can see them.

Then you can take up the cards, shuffle them, and play again.

Here are two extensions of this game. My advice would be to not play all these versions of the game during the same session. It will take some time to memorize the Beatitudes in their entirety. Saving a couple of fresh wrinkles for subsequent sessions will keep the memorization process a little fresher.

Extension 1: Play the Beatitude Buddies game as outlined above. Once the children have found their buddies and spoken aloud their beatitude, have all the children as a group put the Beatitudes in the correct order. They can simply form one long line across the room. Once they are in the correct order according to the Scripture, have Pair 1 recite their beatitude, followed by Pair 2, and so on, until

the entire beatitude has been recited. If you have fewer than eighteen children in the room, you may need to have some pairs recite more than one of the Beatitudes.

Extension 2: Play the Beatitude Buddies game up to the point where the children find their buddies. But instead of having them recite their beatitudes aloud, have them work together quietly. Each pair must develop a very simple ten-seconds-or-less pantomime of their beatitude. After a few minutes, bring all the children together. Then one at a time, have the pairs stand and perform their pantomime. The others must guess which beatitude is being pantomimed.

Memorizing the Beatitudes in their entirety won't happen in the blink of an eye. It will most likely take several sessions. But by offering multiple ways to internalize the Beatitudes—writing them, reading them, hearing them read, playing games about them, acting them out—the children stand a much better chance. Just remember to keep things fresh and keep it moving. Once it starts to feel stale, add a new wrinkle or move on to another activity altogether.

• For Reflection

Ask: Has there ever been a time in your life when the words of the Beatitudes would have been comforting? Without naming names, can you think of someone who might be reassured by this Scripture right now?

Words of Celebration

The people who walked in darkness have seen a great light;
those who lived in a land of deep darkness—on them light has shined.

Isaiah 9:2

• Activity—Cue the Lights!
Supplies: Bibles

Have the children sit with you in a circle on the floor. Practice reciting the Scripture in call-and-response form.

> **You:** The people who walked in darkness
> **Children:** have seen a great light;
> **You:** those who lived in a land of deep darkness—
> **Children:** on them light has shined.

Next, have half the children say the call and the other half the response. Then have the halves switch roles. Finally, have all the children recite the entire Scripture.

Next, have the children stand up. Instruct them that when the lights are off, they must frown, walk slowly, with shoulders stooped, and speak in melancholy tones. When the lights come on, they are to smile, walk briskly or hop, stand up straight, and speak cheerfully.

Turn off the lights and have the children begin moving and reciting the Scripture. When the Scripture gets to "have seen a great light," turn the lights on. Turn the lights back off at "those who lived in a land of deep darkness" and then turn the lights back on at "on them light has shined."

As long as time (and lack of boredom) allows, invite children to be in charge of the lights.

• For Reflection
Ask: Have you ever waited a very long time for something special like Christmas morning or a birthday party, and it felt like the time would never arrive? What's the longest you ever remember waiting for something like that?

Words of Comfort

Come to me, all you that are weary
and are carrying heavy burdens, and I will give you rest.
Matthew 11:28

• Activity—Carrying the Burden

Supplies: Bibles, seven shoeboxes, seven index cards, markers, tape

You will need seven shoeboxes or some other kind of small boxes. Have the children use seven index cards and markers to write the Scripture.

Card 1 — *Come to me,*   **Card** 5 — *heavy burdens,*
Card 2 — *all you*   **Card** 6 — *and I will*
Card 3 — *that are weary*   **Card** 7 — *give you rest.*
Card 4 — *and are carrying*

Tape a card to the side of each box. Distribute the boxes to seven children and have them spread out around the room.

Choose one child (who is not holding a box) to be the "burden carrier."

The child holding Box 1 (*Come to me,*) recites just that fragment of Scripture. The carrier goes over and takes that box.

At that point, the child holding Box 2 (*all you*) recites just that fragment of Scripture. The carrier walks over and the child places Box 2 on top of Box 1.

Continue this until all seven boxes have been placed one on top of the other.

Then have the carrier walk the entire length of the room, balancing all seven boxes, as the other children recite the entire passage of Matthew 11:28.

Then take the boxes, redistribute them, choose a new carrier, and play again. Allow each child to be the burden carrier.

• For Reflection

Ask: Have you ever felt so exhausted that you didn't think you could take another step? How would it feel to have someone pick you up and carry you?

Words of Inspiration

No one has ever seen God; if we love one another,
God lives in us, and his love is perfected in us.

1 John 4:12

• Activity—Telephone

Supplies: Bibles

Yes, the classic game Telephone. This is a great game for memorizing Scripture, provided they are short passages. I doubt Jesus' Sermon on the Mount would make it all the way around the circle.

Have the children sit with you on the floor in a circle. Without introducing the Scripture to the entire group, whisper the Scripture clearly to the child on your right. This child must whisper the Scripture to the child on her or his right, and so on.

Once the Scripture has made it all the way around the circle, the last child (who should be immediately to your left) says what he or she believes to be the Scripture out loud. If it is correct, that's deserving of a BIG celebration. But more than likely, even with one verse of Scripture, it won't have made it all the way around the circle without some changes.

If that is the case, simply say, "That's close, but it's not quite right. Let's try again."

This time, skip the child immediately to your right, and start with the next child. Continue this pattern until the Scripture makes it, reasonably intact, all the way around the circle. I choose not to quibble over tiny deviations.

If you feel that the circle is simply too big, consider dividing it into two smaller circles.

If you have had several tries, but still can't seem to get the correct Scripture all the way around the circle, it's possible that there is one child who may be having difficulty. You may want to walk around the circle and listen in. If one child seems to be struggling, gently help this child and even speak it with her or him.

• For Reflection

Ask: What is something you can do today to show God's love?

Words of Wisdom

Those who oppress the poor insult their Maker,
but those who are kind to the needy honor him.
                                        Proverbs 14:31

• Activity—Musical Shares
Supplies: Bibles, chairs, CD player and CD or MP3 player

This is a cooperative version of Musical Chairs. Set up several chairs in the center of the room in a tight circle facing outward. Have one less chair than the number of children in the room.

Use a CD player, MP3 player, or other music system to play music.

Instruct the children to walk around the circle of chairs, and when the music stops, find a place to sit.

Start the music. The children walk around the chairs. Stop the music when you wish. The children scramble for seats. There will be one standing child who does not have a chair of her or his own. So far, this is played just like Musical Chairs. But here comes the twist.

Say: Hmm, I was sure I had enough places for everyone to sit. Children, why don't you help me figure this out. How can we make room for everyone?

With any luck, one of the children will slide over in her or his chair a little for the standing child to have a place. Otherwise, you may need to suggest it.

Say: That's it! I knew there was enough room for everyone. Sometimes when we help those in need, we have to give up a little of our own comfort. But it's worth it to know that no one is being left out.

Next, take up one of the chairs, but keep all the kids in, and play another round. See how few chairs you can get away with using.

By the way, you may need to specifically encourage side-by-side seating. I'm not a big fan of kids sitting in each others' laps. There's just no need to go there.

• For Reflection
Ask: What can you do to help someone in need?

Words of Jesus

*For he makes his sun rise on the evil and on the good,
and sends rain on the righteous and on the unrighteous.*
Matthew 5:45

• Activity—Hot Potato
Supplies: Bibles, ball or beanbag

Have all the children stand with you in a circle.

Speak through the Scripture a few times.

Begin the game of Hot Potato by passing a ball or beanbag around the circle as the children speak the Scripture in unison. Whoever is holding the ball when the Scripture gets to the word "unrighteous," must call out, "Matthew five, verse forty-five!"

Then that child starts the next game of Hot Potato. Playing this cooperative version allows all the children to keep repeating the verse, rather than having those children who are "in" and those who are "out."

After a few rounds, play the game using the word "righteous" as the keyword. Whoever is holding the ball when the Scripture gets to the word "righteous," must call out, "Matthew five, verse forty-five!"

• For Reflection
Ask: When was the last time something happened to you that wasn't fair? When has something unfair worked in your favor?

For he makes his sun rise on the evil and on the good, and sends rain on the righteous and on the unrighteous.

Matthew 5:45

Brown Belt Level

The Big Thing: Bible Black Belts Pledge; Parables—The Sower and the Seeds (Luke 8:5-8), The Lost Coin (Luke 15:8-10), The House on the Rock (Matthew 7:24-27), The Mustard Seed (Matthew 13:31-32), The Good Samaritan (Luke 10:30-37). **Choose two.**

Words of Celebration: Job 19:25

Words of Comfort: John 16:33

Words of Inspiration: Hebrews 11:1

Words of Wisdom: 1 Corinthians 13:13

Words of Jesus: Matthew 6:21

The Parable of the Sower and the Seeds—A sower went out to sow his seed; and as he sowed, some fell on the path and was trampled on, and the birds of the air ate it up. Some fell on the rock; and as it grew up, it withered for lack of moisture. Some fell among thorns, and the thorns grew with it and choked it. Some fell into good soil, and when it grew, it produced a hundredfold. (Luke 8:5-8)

The Parable of the Lost Coin—Or what woman having ten silver coins, if she loses one of them, does not light a lamp, sweep the house, and search carefully until she finds it? When she has found it, she calls together her friends and neighbors, saying, "Rejoice with me, for I have found the coin that I had lost." Just so, I tell you, there is joy in the presence of the angels of God over one sinner who repents. (Luke 15:8-10)

The Parable of the House Built on the Rock—Everyone then who hears these words of mine and acts on them will be like a wise man who built his house on the rock. The rain fell, the floods came, and the winds blew and beat on that house, but it did not fall, because it had been founded on rock. And everyone who hears these words of mine and does not act on them will be like a foolish man who built his house on sand. The rain fell, and the floods came, and the winds blew and beat against that house, and it fell—and great was its fall! (Matthew 7:24-27)

The Parable of the Mustard Seed—He put before them another parable: "The kingdom of heaven is like a mustard seed that someone took and sowed in his field; it is the smallest of all the seeds, but when it has grown it is the greatest of shrubs and becomes a tree, so that the birds of the air come and make nests in its branches." (Matthew 13:31-32)

The Parable of the Good Samaritan—Jesus replied, "A man was going down from Jerusalem to Jericho, and fell into the hands of robbers, who stripped him, beat him, and went away, leaving him half dead. Now by chance a priest was going down that road; and when he saw him, he passed by on the other side. So likewise a Levite, when he came to the place and saw him, passed by on the other side. But a Samaritan while traveling came near him; and when he saw him, he was moved with pity. He went to him and bandaged his wounds, having poured oil and wine on them. Then he put him on his own animal, brought him to an inn, and took care of him. The next day he took out two denarii, gave them to the innkeeper, and said, 'Take care of him; and when I come back, I will repay you whatever more you spend.' Which of these three, do you think, was a neighbor to the man who fell into the hands of the robbers?" He said, "The one who showed him mercy." Jesus said to him, "Go and do likewise." (Luke 10:30-37)

A few things about the parables. The children do not have to memorize all five parables. Yikes! That would take months. Allow each child to choose two that he or she will learn well. And notice that I said "learn well" and not memorize. Since these passages are so long, I am more concerned with the children having the right people or objects go through the right events in the right sequence. If they miss a word here or there, it's no big deal. I want them to get the gist of each parable.

Speaking of getting the gist—these parables are concrete in their own right. The objects and actions are simple and memorable. What can make these parables tricky, especially for younger children, is that they represent something else. "The kingdom of heaven is like . . ." "God's love is like . . ." "The seed is the word of God." This requires kids to make the leap from concrete object to abstract metaphor, and that's a big leap. Older children are certainly developing in this area, but when it comes to the younger children, I try to use "like" and "as" sparingly.

That said, these are amazing teaching stories that have lasted for two thousand years. At this point in our kids' lives, I'm not sure it's 100% vital for them to understand every nuance of these parables just yet. The children have the rest of their lives to unpack all the rich content in these parables. For now it is enough for them to be able to know and retell these amazing stories.

The Big Thing

Bible Black Belts Pledge
Say the **Bible Black Belts Pledge** (page 15).

• Activity—Storyboards
Supplies: Bibles, card stock, pencils, crayons or markers

Divide the children into five groups. Give each group four sheets of white card stock, pencils, and an assortment of crayons or markers.

Assign a different parable to each group. Their task is to tell the story using a sequence of pictures. They are not allowed to use any written words. Each parable must be conveyed using pictures only.

Encourage the children to plan out their storyboards before they start coloring. They only have four panels on which to tell the entire story.

Once the children have finished the storyboards, invite each group to present its work to the others.

A simple and fun game to play is to have a group show their panels, but out of order. The other children must put the pictures in the correct sequence.

Do this for each of the parables.

Once the session is over, you may display the storyboards on the wall for the rest of the month or year.

Another good reason to hold on to the storyboards is for later assessment. Some children may find it very difficult to verbally recount the people, objects, and events of a parable. Allow these children to use the storyboards to demonstrate their comprehension of the proper sequence.

• Activity—Living Pictures
Supplies: Bibles

The French term for this is *tableaux vivants*. This is a combination of visual art and theatre.

Divide the children into five groups.

Assign a different parable to each group.

Each group must come up with three to four tableaux, or living pictures, to depict their assigned parable. The children can portray the different people or objects in the parables.

They can arrange themselves as one of the living pictures, and then they must freeze in place for five seconds before moving on to the next living picture.

Make sure the children remember to organize their living pictures to reflect the correct sequence of the parable.

Once the groups have created their series of living pictures, invite the groups to perform their living pictures for the others.

Think of this activity as storyboards in 3-D. Once all the groups have performed their living pictures, you can have them play a game where a group performs its pictures out of sequence, and the others have to determine the correct order.

• **For Reflection:**
   Ask: Think of a character you admire from a book (not the Bible). What do you admire most about that character?

Words of Celebration

For I know that my Redeemer lives,
and that at the last he will stand upon the earth.
Job 19:25

• Activity—Scripture Tag Team

Supplies: Bibles

Divide the children into pairs.

Have one child in each pair start reciting the Scripture. Then at any moment, that child may tag the partner's hand and the partner must continue the Scripture wherever the first child left off.

The tagging can continue back and forth.

This activity works well for any Scripture. It works great for long passages because it allows for a lot of tagging.

Modify this activity for shorter passages by having the tag teams go through the Scripture several times.

• For Reflection

Ask: How do you think Jesus' friends felt when he died? How do you think they felt when they saw him alive again? How do you feel knowing that Jesus lives and loves us right now—today?

Words of Comfort

I have said this to you, so that in me you may have peace.
In the world you face persecution.
But take courage; I have conquered the world!

John 16:33

• Activity—One-Minute Marathon

Supplies: Bibles, posterboard, crayons, masking tape

Divide the children into five groups. Give each group one sheet of posterboard and an assortment of crayons. Each group must write part of the Scripture on their signs.

Sign 1 — *I have said this to you,*
Sign 2 — *so that in me you may have peace.*
Sign 3 — *In the world you face persecution.*
Sign 4 — *But take courage;*
Sign 5 — *I have conquered the world!*

While some are working on the lettering for the signs, others in each group can decorate the signs with pictures or symbols. Encourage the children to write as legibly as possible.

Once the signs have been created, take them up, along with the crayons. Tape each of the signs in a different part of the room.

Make sure the floor is clear of any obstructions.

Use tape to mark a start line on the floor, and again to mark a finish line.

Here is how the One-Minute Marathon works.

Have the children get ready at the start line.

On your signal, they begin by running in place for sixteen steps (for John 16). Then they hop to the first sign and read it aloud. Then they run in place for sixteen more steps, and so on.

After they have read the last sign, they must run in place for sixteen more steps before hopping across the finish line. Once they cross the finish line, they must recite the entire Scripture. It's okay for them to use the signs as an aid.

The goal is to finish in less than one minute. Depending on the size of the group (not to mention the size of the room), you may need to divide the children into several small groups. That would be a good way to give each child a rest between marathons. Allow each child to run the marathon two or three times.

By the way, any time I've tried to run a long distance, I ALWAYS felt like I was running in place!

• For Reflection

Ask: What's the longest you could run at one try? What's the longest you could pray at one sitting?

Words of Inspiration

Now faith is the assurance of things hoped for,
the conviction of things not seen.

Hebrews 11:1

• Activity—Marco Polo
Supplies: Bibles

This game is a variation on the swimming game Marco Polo. In Marco Polo, one person closes her or his eyes and calls out "Marco!" All the other swimmers must reply "Polo!" The person with the closed eyes tries to tag one of the other swimmers, using only sound.

Here's how this game works. First, clear an open space in the room. Eliminate hard edges and corners. If there is some immovable object in the room, such as a very heavy table, just stand next to it to act as a buffer. Your job is to keep the game fun AND safe.

Choose one child to be "IT." This child will close her or his eyes and call out, "Hebrews 11!" Every time this is called out, the other children must reply, "Verse 1!" The child whose eyes are closed must use the sound of the replies to find and tag one of the other children. But the game doesn't end here!

Once a child is tagged, the one who is IT must recite the first half of the Scripture, "Now faith is the assurance of things hoped for . . ." The tagged child must reply, ". . . the conviction of things not seen."

At that point, the child who is IT may open her or his eyes. Then all the children recite the Scripture one time. The tagged child becomes IT, and the group plays another round.

Here are some ways to modify the game to make it less active. You can have the IT child close her or his eyes. Then the other children get to go find a spot, but once they've found one, they must stay put. Another way to adapt can be to allow the children to try to escape the IT child, but only by walking or hopping on one leg.

• For Reflection
Ask: What are some things in our world that we know exist, even though we can't see them? *(air, neutrons, smells, and so on)* What is something you have faith in, even though you have never seen it with your eyes?

Brown Belt Level **97**

Words of Wisdom

And now faith, hope, and love abide, these three; and the greatest of these is love.
1 Corinthians 13:13

• Activity—Body Ostinato
Supplies: Bibles

Ostinato is a musical term similar to the word *obstinate*—something that is played or sung over and over again. But don't worry. You don't need to be a Mozart to perform this ostinato. It's very simple. You touch your toes, then your knees, then your waist, then your shoulders, then your head, and back down the same way. Just keep the movement at a steady pace.

Toes-Knees-Waist-Shoulders-Head-Shoulders-Waist-Knees Toes-Knees-Waist-Shoulders-Head-Shoulders-Waist-Knees and so on.

Have the children spread out so they all have plenty of room. Have them recite 1 Corinthians 13:13 a few times.

Next, have the children just perform the body ostinato. Then put the two together.

faith,		hope,	and		love	a-		bide,	these	three;
Toes Knees		*Waist*	*Shoulders*		*Head*	*Shoulders*		*Waist*	*Knees*	*Toes*

and		the		greatest		of	these		is	love.
Knees		*Waist*		*Shoulders*		*Head*	*Shoulders*		*Waist*	*Knees.*

When you get back down to Toes, you can end, or do the entire ostinato again.

Once the kids get really good, try going a bit faster.

• For Reflection
Ask: Why is love the greatest of these?

Words of Jesus

For where your treasure is, there your heart will be also.
Matthew 6:21

• Activity—Treasure Hunt
Supplies: Bibles, shoebox, index card, marker

Before the session, decorate a shoebox to look like a treasure chest. Actually, all you really need is the shoebox; the imagination of the children can do the rest. Inside the box, place an index card with the Scripture written on it.

Select one child to close her or his eyes. This child will be the treasure hunter.

Then select another child to hide the shoebox somewhere in the room.

Once that has been done, invite the hunter to open her or his eyes and begin looking for the box. When the hunter gets closer, the other children are to say, "Arr!" And when the hunter gets farther away, the children are to say, "Shiver me timbers." (The more pirate-y, the better.) When the hunter finally finds the box, he or she must open it and read the index card aloud. Then all the children must say the Scripture together.

Repeat this game several times. If there is enough time, allow each child a chance to hide the treasure and a chance to hunt for it.

• For Reflection
Ask: When was the last time you bought or made something just for you? When was the last time you bought or made something for someone else?

Black Belt Level

The Big Thing: Bible Black Belts Pledge, The Lord's Prayer (Matthew 6:9-13, KJV)

Words of Celebration: Psalm 150:6

Words of Comfort: Psalm 46:10

Words of Inspiration: Micah 6:8

Words of Wisdom: Proverbs 16:32

Words of Jesus: Matthew 18:21-22

The Lord's Prayer

Our Father which art in heaven, hallowed be thy name.
Thy kingdom come. Thy will be done in earth, as it is in heaven.
Give us this day our daily bread.
And forgive us our debts, as we forgive our debtors.
And lead us not into temptation, but deliver us from evil.

(Matthew 6:9-13, KJV)

We chose the Matthew version because it more closely reflects the traditional Lord's Prayer we use in worship. The other version is found in Luke 11:2-4.

It is also worth noting that the phrase, "For thine is the kingdom and the power and the glory forever," is not originally found in either Matthew's or Luke's account. It was added many years later.

The Big Thing

Bible Black Belts Pledge
Say the **Bible Black Belts Pledge** (page 15).

• Activity—Hand Prayer
Supplies: Bibles

This is a more contemplative yet still physical activity. Invite each child to find a nice quiet spot in the room, giving one another plenty of space. Recite the Lord's Prayer for them, as it appears in Matthew. At that point, some of the children may notice that the "For thine is the kingdom . . ." section was left out. Explain to them that this section is known as the doxology (words of praise) of the Lord's Prayer and was added many years later.

Invite each of the children to hold out one hand.

Say: Just as a hand has five fingers, there are five sections to the Lord's Prayer.

Lead the children through the reciting of the Lord's Prayer while using the five fingers to track each of the sections of the prayer.

> **Thumb** — *Our Father which art in heaven, hallowed be thy name.*
> **Index Finger** — *Thy kingdom come. Thy will be done in earth, as it is in heaven.*
> **Middle Finger** — *Give us this day our daily bread.*
> **Ring Finger** — *And forgive us our debts, as we forgive our debtors.*
> **Pinkie** — *And lead us not into temptation, but deliver us from evil.*

The children can track the sections of the prayer by using the opposite hand to hold on to the corresponding finger for each section.

For a follow-up activity, have each of the children take a turn touching a finger while the other children respond with the corresponding section. Modify for children without five fingers by using leg, arm, head, arm, leg.

• For Reflection
Ask: Outside of this room, when have you prayed the Lord's Prayer? Are there times when knowing the Lord's Prayer could help you get through a difficult situation? Create your own prayer using your five fingers to keep track of the different parts.

Words of Celebration

Let everything that breathes praise the LORD! Praise the LORD!

Psalm 150:6

• Activity—Even-Count Belly-Breathing
Supplies: Bibles

How often do we remember to breathe? I don't mean just inhale and exhale, I mean really breathe. On stressful days or during busy times of the church year, I can go entire days without stopping to take a good, deep, replenishing breath.

Invite the children to each find a quiet spot in the room where they can sit. Have them make sure to give one another plenty of space.

Then have the children recite Psalm 150:6.

Immediately following this, have the children inhale for three counts, then exhale for three counts. You be the one to count, in a gentle, soothing voice.

Repeat this activity, always starting by reciting the Scripture together.

Encourage the children to breathe deeply, so that they feel as if their bellies are expanding slightly. If you've ever watched a sleeping baby, you know what this looks like. For many of us, the breath seems to "get stuck" in our shoulders or the upper part of the chest. But when we are breathing naturally and openly, each breath goes all the way down.

After a few times counting to three, try breathing in and out on counts of four, five, or even six.

This activity can be a good all-the-time activity, not just as a one-shot activity to help the children with this one passage of Scripture. We all need to be reminded from time to time about the importance of true breathing.

• For Reflection
Ask: When was the last time you felt really stressed out about something? Can you think of any stressful times ahead when remembering this Scripture could be helpful?

Words of Comfort

Be still, and know that I am God!
Psalm 46:10

• Activity—A Call to Stillness
Supplies: Bibles

This is a simple, and valuable, activity that you can use throughout the year. *Bible Black Belts* is highly active. From time to time, you may find that the room is perhaps a bit too active (or loud). Teach the children this simple call-and-response to help get their attention and bring stillness to the room.

Instruct the children that no matter what they are doing, whenever they hear you say, "Be still and know," they are to stop what they are doing and respond, "that I am God!" Then they must either stand or sit in silence and wait for further instruction from you.

As you can see, this activity can be beneficial all year, not just during the training for one particular belt.

As the year progresses, modify the activity. Have your call be, "Psalm forty-six, verse ten," to which the children respond, "Be still, and know that I am God!"

Don't forget to allow for at least a few seconds of silence and stillness. Don't feel that once the room is still you must immediately jump into the next activity.

• For Reflection
Ask: When are some times when you find it very difficult to be still? Are there times or places in your life you wish were more still? Where? When? How can we connect with God when we move? How can we connect with God when we're still?

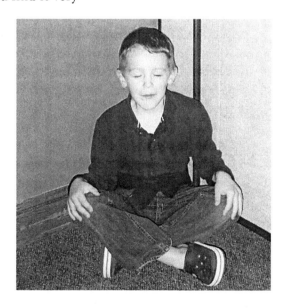

Words of Inspiration

What does the LORD require of you but to do justice,
and to love kindness, and to walk humbly with your God?

Micah 6:8

• Activity—Reaction

Supplies: Bibles

This is a fun and very physical game.

Have the children stand with you in a circle. Make sure everyone has plenty of space around them.

Teach the children four simple actions that correspond with different parts of the Scripture.

> **What does the LORD require of you** — *Hold your hands together over your head in "praying hands" position.*
> **Do justice** — *Hold your hands out to either side, palms up. Then move your hands up and down, as if weighing things on either side like a scale.*
> **Love kindness** — *Place both hands over your heart.*
> **Walk humbly with your God** — *Walk in place.*

Instruct the children that every time they hear a phrase from the Scripture, they must perform the corresponding motion.

Start slowly at first. Call out a phrase, and then another. It is not necessary to keep the phrases in the same order as they appear in the Scripture. Just make sure all the children are performing the proper motions for each phrase. It all seems pretty easy at first. But gradually call out the phrases faster and faster.

If there is time, let each child have a chance to lead by calling out phrases. Each time you switch leaders, have the entire group recite the Scripture in the proper order.

• For Reflection:

Ask: Have you ever felt that you were asked to do more than you could handle?
Do you think God ever asks us to do more than we can handle?

Words of Wisdom

One who is slow to anger is better than the mighty,
and one whose temper is controlled than one who captures a city.

Proverbs 16:32

• Activity—Slo-Mo

Supplies: Bibles

Invite the children to move about the room as they recite the Scripture in unison. They may walk, hop, swing their arms, make swimming motions, or anything else that is safe and doesn't distract others.

Next have the children recite the Scripture again in slow motion as they make the same motions as before, all in slow motion.

Try it again in super slow motion.

• For Reflection

Ask: When was the last time you were really angry? Did you act out of that anger right away or did you wait? Which way do you feel is better? Are there ever times when it's okay to be angry?

Words of Jesus

Then Peter came and said to him, "Lord, if another member of the church sins against me, how often should I forgive?
As many as seven times?" Jesus said to him,
"Not seven times, but I tell you, seventy-seven times."

Matthew 18:21-22

(Note: some versions use "seventy times seven.")

• Activity—Marbles
Supplies: Bibles, large container of marbles (or pebbles)

Before introducing this Scripture, have the children sit in a circle. Walk around the circle with the container of marbles. Invite each child to reach in with one hand and take as many as he or she likes.

Say: I would like each of you to think about someone who has recently hurt your feelings or treated you unfairly—no names, please. Does everybody have a person in mind? *(Give them a few seconds before going on.)* Now here's what I want you to do: for every marble you have, I want you to think of something nice about that person.

This may be met with more than just a little resistance, if not laughter. Is it a big deal if they took twelve marbles, but can only think of seven nice things? No. Just like it's not that big a difference whether it's seventy-seven times or seventy times seven. It's about humanizing the other person. It's easy to resent someone when we only see the negative. But it gets harder to keep resenting that person when we have to admit that, yes, there are some good things about him or her. In fact, we might just have to forgive that person.

One at a time, have the children put the marbles back into the container. Each time a child puts her or his marbles back, have the entire group say the Scripture. You may have to read it aloud the first few times. Then invite the children to join you as they catch on. At the close of the session, allow each child to take a marble home as a reminder that they have the power to forgive.

• For Reflection
Ask: Can you think of someone you have recently had a hard time forgiving for something? How might this Scripture help you work through that?

Then Peter came and
said to him,
"Lord, if another
member of the church
sins against me, how
often should I forgive?
As many as
seven times?"
Jesus said to him,
"Not seven times,
but I tell you,
seventy-seven times."

Matthew 18:21-22

Just for Fun—Just in Case

Perhaps the kids have been working hard on memorizing the Beatitudes. Or maybe they're having a hard time keeping Philippians and Philemon straight. Whatever the case, you can see that they just need a break from whatever it is they're doing so that they can come back to it refreshed and excited, rather than frustrated.

• Activity—B-I-B-L-E

This is a simple activity that gets the heart pumping, the blood flowing, and really takes the edge off. It's also a great activity for waking up when the children seem to come in a little more tired and sluggish than normal.

Here's how it works.

Have the children stand with you. Raise your left hand overhead and shake it five times as you all call out, very loudly, "B-I-B-L-E."

Immediately go to the right hand, shake it five times, and call, "B-I-B-L-E."

Then do the same for the left and right foot.

Without skipping a beat, go back to the left hand and shake it four times as you call out, "B-I-B-L."

Continue with the right hand, left foot, and right foot.

Then shake the left hand three times as you call out, "B-I-B."

You get the idea.

By the end, you are all shaking each hand and foot only one time.

Everyone laughs. Heart rates are up. Spirits are up. And minds are more open and alert.

Your word is a lamp to my feet and a light to my path.

Psalm 119:105

Review

• **Review Activity—Four Walls**
Supplies: posterboard, marker, tape

Beatitudes. Commandments. Old Testament. New Testament. Parables. The children are going to have A LOT of Scripture bouncing around in those brilliant brains of theirs. So it's good to have activities for keeping things straight. Four Walls is a fun game that can help. On each of the four walls in your room, put up a sign with a category.

> For example:
> **Wall 1:** *Books of the Old Testament*
> **Wall 2:** *The Beatitudes*
> **Wall 3:** *Books of the New Testament*
> **Wall 4:** *The Ten Commandments*

Have the children stand in the center of the room and listen carefully as you call out something that would belong in one of the four categories. The children must indicate which category by going and touching the wall with the sign for that particular category.

For example, if you call out, "You shall not steal," the children must go and touch the wall with the Ten Commandments sign on it. Then have the children come back to the center of the room. Have the children hop, moonwalk, or walk in slow motion to the walls.

Here are some things you can call out for the categories listed above, with the correct category in parentheses.

1. **You shall not kill.** *(Ten Commandments)*
2. **Joshua** *(Books of the Old Testament)*
3. **Jude** *(Books of the New Testament)*
4. **You shall have no gods before me.** *(Ten Commandments)*
5. **Blessed are the merciful, for they will receive mercy.**
   (The Beatitudes)
6. **2 Chronicles** *(Books of the Old Testament)*
7. **2 Corinthians** *(Books of the New Testament)*
8. **1 Corinthians** *(Books of the New Testament)*
9. **1 Chronicles** *(Books of the Old Testament)*
(Yes, those four books are grouped like that on purpose.)
10. **You shall not tell lies about others.** *(Ten Commandments)*
11. **Blessed are the peacemakers, for they will be called children of God.**
    (The Beatitudes)
12. **Honor your father and mother.** *(Ten Commandments)*
13. **Malachi** *(Books of the Old Testament)*
14. **Esther** *(Books of the Old Testament)*

15. Blessed are the poor in spirit, for theirs is the kingdom of heaven. *(The Beatitudes)*
16. **Romans** *(Books of the New Testament)*
17. **You shall not make and worship idols.** *(Ten Commandments)*
18. **Luke** *(Books of the New Testament)*
19. **Jeremiah** *(Books of the Old Testament)*
20. **Blessed are the meek, for they will inherit the earth.** *(The Beatitudes)*

You can also switch out the categories. Some other categories could include Psalms, Proverbs, Parables, Epistles (Letters), and the Lord's Prayer.

•Review Activity—In a Flash
Supplies: Bibles, index cards, markers

Very often children can memorize an entire verse or set of verses. But when asked to give the Scripture reference, they often forget where the Scripture came from. (I can tell you all Ten Commandments, but when it comes to the exact chapter and verses, well . . . can I get back to you on that?)

This activity will help children find all those Bible verses so they can share them with their families and friends.

Prepare several index cards as flash cards, each with a different Scripture reference on it. These need to be Scriptures that the children have learned. On the back of each card, have the actual passage written out.

Have the children stand in front of you. Hold up a flash card, showing a Scripture reference. The children must try to say that Scripture.

For example, if you hold up a card labeled Philippians 4:4, the children should say, "Rejoice in the Lord always; again I will say, Rejoice." (You can check it using the back of the card.)

Better still, have the children make the flash cards. First of all, this gives them the chance to write the Scriptures, which will help with memorization. Second, it keeps you from having to stay up late Saturday night making sets. And third, with multiple sets, you can divide the children into smaller groups so that each child gets more "reps."

A few suggestions:
1. Keep the Scriptures short. Don't have a child write the entire Peaceable Kingdom on the back of an index card.
2. Encourage the children to write legibly.
3. Play this game in the last session of each belt level, and only use the Scriptures the children have already experienced.
4. The children can also reverse the game, seeing the entire Scripture on the flash card and having to give the reference.
5. Make sure that within each small group the children take turns showing the flash cards and reciting the Scripture or Scripture reference.

Scripture Index

Scripture Index